DRAFT

MATTAMUSKEET NATIONAL WILDLIFE REFUGE COMPLEX

Mattamuskeet National Wildlife Refuge
Swanquarter National Wildlife Refuge
Cedar Island National Wildlife Refuge

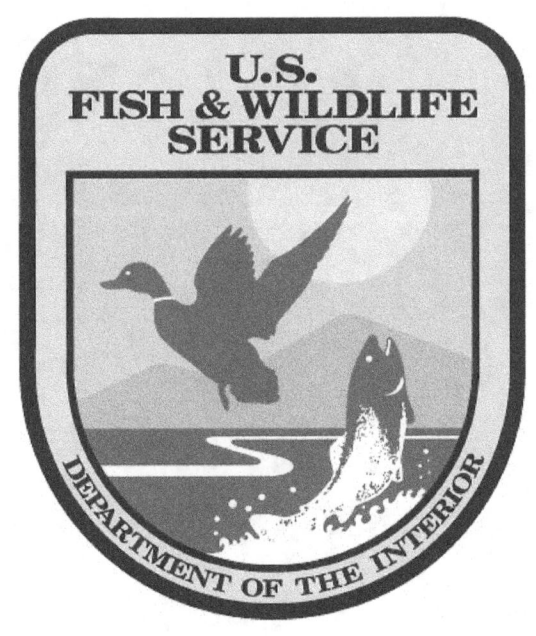

FIRE MANAGEMENT PLAN

July 2009

Fire Management Plan

Mattamuskeet National Wildlife Refuge Complex

Prepared: _____   **Date:** _____

  Arthur D. Latterell, Fire Mgmt. Planner
  Wildland Fire Associates L.L.C.

Reviewed: _____   **Date:** _____

  Thomas G. Crews, Jr.
  Fire Management Officer, District 1

Reviewed: _____   **Date:** _____

  Bruce Freske, Refuge Manager
  Mattamuskeet Refuge Complex

Reviewed: _____   **Date:** _____

  Bob Eaton, Regional Fire Mgmt. Coordinator
  Southeast Region, U.S. Fish & Wildlife Service

Reviewed: _____   **Date:** _____

  Pete Jerome, Refuge Supervisor, Area 3
  Southeast Region, U.S. Fish & Wildlife Service

Reviewed: _____   **Date:** _____

  John Andrew, Regional Chief, Refuges
  Southeast Region, U.S. Fish & Wildlife Service

Approved: _____   **Date:** _____

  Sam Hamliton, Regional Director
  Southeast Region, U.S. Fish & Wildlife Service

Table of Contents

List of Tables

List of Figures

List of Appendices

A. Fire Operations
   1. FWS-NCDFR Cooperative Plan (Annual Operations Plan)
   2. Regional Dispatch Plan
   3. District 1 Step-up Plan
   4. Fire Card
B. Aviation
   1.1. Station Aviation Plans
   1.2. Air Operations Addendum to Annual Prescribed Fire Plans
   2. Pre-Accident Plan
C. Medical Dispatch Plan
D. Fire Transitional Documents
E. Pre-Attack Plan
   1. Vendors List
   2. Extended Attack Organization
   3.1. Mattamuskeet Values to Protect Map
   3.2. Swanquarter Values to Protect Map
   3.3. Cedar Island Values to Protect Map
   4. Endangered Species Considerations
F. Standard Operating Procedures for Safety
G. Delegation for District 1 FMO
H. Fire Staffing Plan
   1. District 1 Approved Fire Staffing Chart
   2. Fire Team Positions and Responsibilities (revised)
   3. District 1 Firefighting Qualifications
I. RXCM Exception
J. Smoke Management Guidelines
   1. State Smoke Management Guidelines
   2. Guidelines for Operational Evaluation Burns
   3. Smoke Hazards Maps
K. Job Hazard Analyses
L. Agreements List
M. (Reserved for Community Wildfire Protection Plans)
N. References and Literature Cited
O. Burn Table
P. Wildfire Table
Q. Annual FMP Review Checklist
R. (Reserved for approved Environmental Assessment)
S. (Reserved for Draft Plan Comments and Service Responses)

1.0 Introduction

1.1. Purpose of the Fire Management Plan (FMP)

This Fire Management Plan documents the objectives, policies, and practices for fire management activities on the Mattamuskeet National Wildlife Refuge Complex (Mattamuskeet Complex). The Mattamuskeet Complex consists of Mattamuskeet National Wildlife Refuge (NWR), Swanquarter NWR and Cedar Island NWR. These refuges are administered by the U.S. Fish and Wildlife Service (Service) of the U.S. Department of the Interior (Department). This plan is written to meet Department and Service requirements that every area with burnable vegetation must have an approved FMP *(620 DM 1.4)*. It enables the Mattamuskeet Complex to meet a Service requirement that Refuges review and/or revise FMPs at a minimum of five-year intervals or when significant land use changes are proposed *(621 FW 2)*.

The goal of wildland fire management is to plan and implement actions that help accomplish the mission of the National Wildlife Refuge System, which is to administer a national network of lands and waters for the conservation, management, and, where appropriate, restoration of the fish, wildlife, and plant resources and their habitats within the United States for the benefit of present and future generations of Americans.

The original FMP for the Mattamuskeet Complex was written in 2001 and is a step-down plan of the refuges' outdated Refuge Management Plans. Mattamuskeet and Swanquarter National Wildlife Refuges both completed their Comprehensive Conservation Plans (CCP) in July 2008 and Cedar Island NWR completed its CCP in September 2006. These CCPs serve as the new foundation for management actions on these refuges.

This FMP integrates all wildland fire management and related activities within the context of the approved CCP. It defines a program to manage wildland fires (wildfire and prescribed fire) and all other aspects of fire management including prevention, fuel treatments, education and outreach, and training to protect values and enhance resources on the refuges within the Complex. The Step-up Plan and Annual Operations Plan (in Appendices) detail preparedness and wildfire response actions to be taken by Refuge staff and cooperators. Together, the FMP and its appendices provide detailed direction for programs to implement fire management policies and objectives on the Mattamuskeet Complex. Its purpose is to assure that wildland fire management goals and components are coordinated between refuge program areas, fire management resources within the District, and with fire management cooperators.

1.2. General Description of the Area in the Fire Management Plan

Northeastern North Carolina is very productive and important for fish and wildlife populations, and includes some of the wildest lands in the mid-Atlantic. Lands within the Mattamuskeet Complex lie in sparsely populated areas of the mid-Atlantic coastal plain along the Atlantic Flyway. The Mattamuskeet Complex headquarters is located on Mattamuskeet NWR in Swan Quarter, North Carolina, approximately 170 miles east of Raleigh. Swanquarter and Cedar Island NWRs are administered as satellite refuges.

Figure 1: USFWS Southeast Region Fire Management District 1

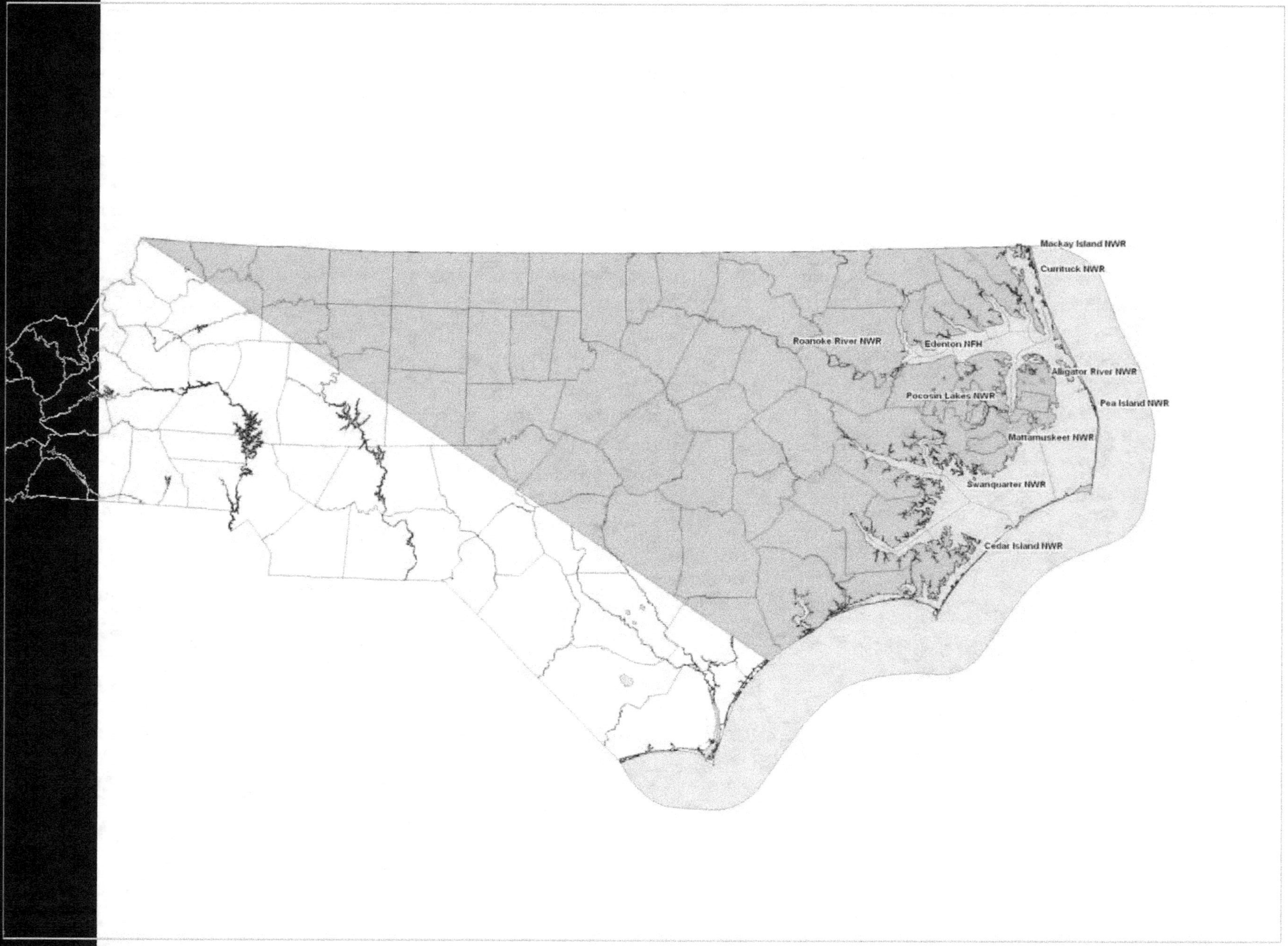

Mackay Island NWR
Currituck NWR
Alligator River NWR
Pea Island NWR
Mattamuskeet NWR
Cedar Island NWR
Edenton NFH
Pocosin Lakes NWR
Swanquarter NWR
Roanoke River NWR

Table 1: Management Units in the Mattamuskeet Fire Management Complex

FWS Management Units within the FMP	Total Acres (Burnable Acres)
Mattamuskeet National Wildlife Refuge	50,180 (10,155)
Swanquarter National Wildlife Refuge	16,411 (16,400)
Cedar Island National Wildlife Refuge	14,480 (14,395)
Total	81,071 (40,950)

Together with six other refuges and the Edenton National Fish Hatchery, the Mattamuskeet Complex makes up Fire District 1 of the Southeast Region of the Service in northeast North Carolina (Figure 1). Although specific to each refuge and a refuge's FMP, much of the fire management operations and planning are done on a District basis. The District fire office is in Manteo, North Carolina at Alligator River NWR.

1.2.1. <u>Mattamuskeet National Wildlife Refuge</u>

Mattamuskeet NWR is located on the Albemarle - Pamlico peninsula in Hyde County, nine miles east of Swan Quarter, NC by U.S. Highways 264 and 94, Mattamuskeet NWR consists of more than 50,000 acres of water, marsh, timber and crop lands. Figure 2 shows a general map of the refuge. Its most significant feature is Lake Mattamuskeet, the largest natural lake in North Carolina (40,000 acres). The value of Lake Mattamuskeet as a resource is directly linked to water quality. The concentrations of wintering waterfowl and the resulting hunting have given the lake national recognition.

While noted for waterfowl, Mattamuskeet NWR also provides habitats for a significant fishery resource, 70-90 pairs of nesting osprey, wintering bald eagles and peregrine falcons, white-tailed deer, bobcats, river otters, gray foxes, 240 bird species, an occasional black bear or endangered red wolf, and numerous other species endemic to the area. It includes 6,425 acres of shallow freshwater marsh, 3,340 acres of wetland forest, 13 moist-soil impoundments and three cropland areas. Public use consists of waterfowl and deer hunting, fishing, crabbing, wildlife viewing, wildlife photography and environmental education,.

The refuge's Comprehensive Conservation Plan (CCP) was completed in July 2008 to guide the management of Mattamuskeet for the next 15-years. Chapter II of the CCP (FWS 2008) includes a thorough description of the physical and biological environments on the refuge and the socioeconomic conditions of the surrounding area. Appendix J of the CCP is a list of refuge biota and includes the common and scientific names for species mentioned in this FMP.

Mattamuskeet Lodge, a pumping plant turned hunting lodge, is listed on the National Register of Historic Places. In 2006, Congress authorized the transfer of the Mattamuskeet Lodge to the State of North Carolina. In this bill, approximately 6 acres of land that included the Lodge and the refuge headquarters area were transferred to the State. There is no approved acquisition boundary for the refuge so there are no inholdings.

Figure 2: Mattamuskeet National Wildlife Refuge – Current Lands

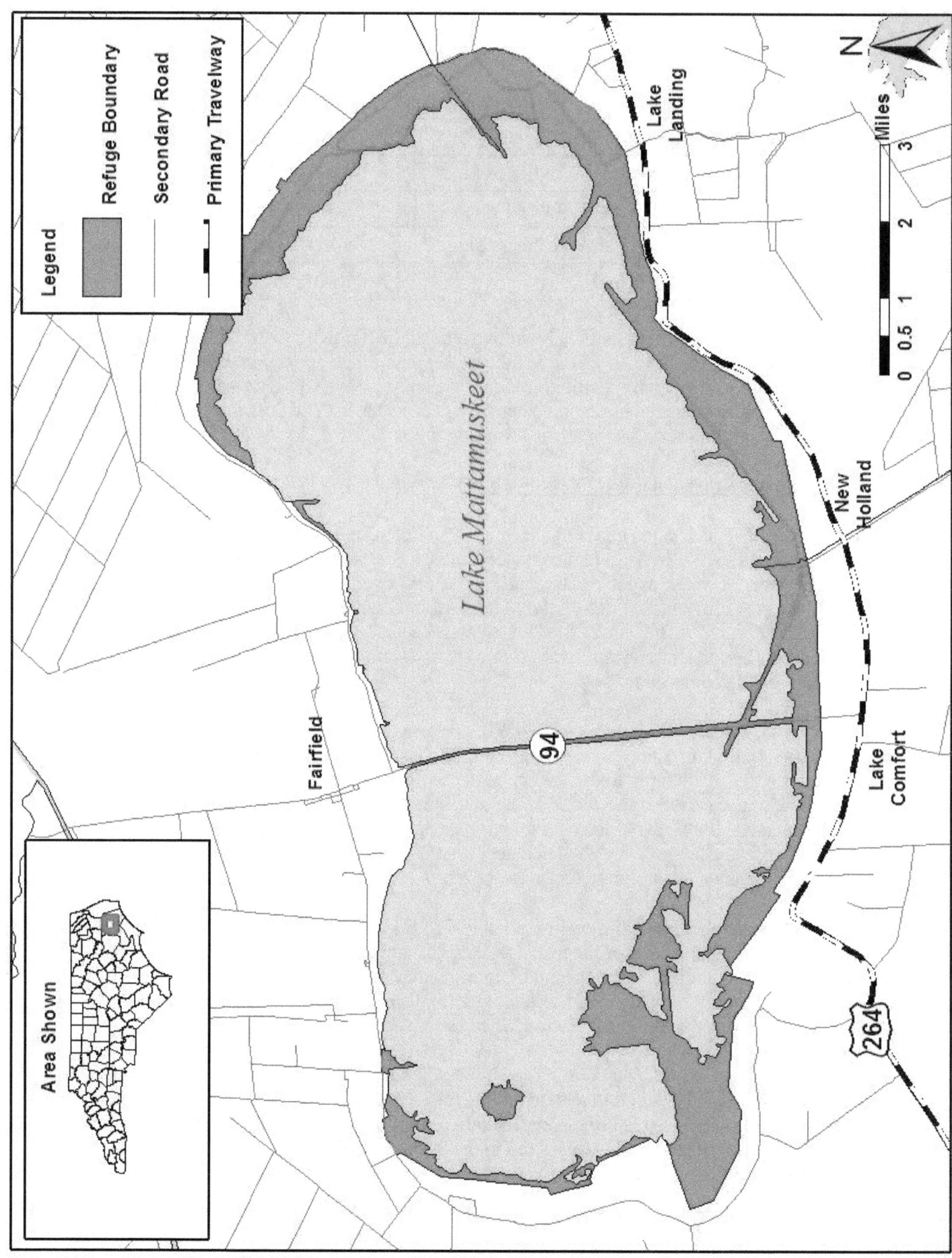

The CCP (FWS 2008) established a vision for the refuge of which the following portions are pertinent to fire management on the refuge:

Mattamuskeet National Wildlife Refuge will function as a vital part of National Wildlife Refuge System to remain a premier wintering area for ducks, geese, and swans on the Atlantic Flyway. The refuge will maintain breeding habitat for a variety of migratory birds, will maintain an extensive network of moist-soil units, and will protect and enhance healthy wetland and aquatic ecosystems, while considering and striving to mitigate the effects of climate change and rising sea levels. It will also protect Service trust species, including threatened and endangered species...The refuge staff will cooperate with partners and volunteers to achieve the refuge's goals. The Fish and Wildlife Service will continue to conduct research in cooperation with government agencies, non-governmental agencies, universities, and others...

1.2.2. Swanquarter National Wildlife Refuge

Swanquarter NWR is located in Hyde County on the north shore of Pamlico Sound east and west of the village of Swan Quarter, NC. The refuge includes 16,411 acres of irregularly-flooded brackish marsh and forested wetlands. A 27,000 acre Presidential Proclamation Area of adjacent Sound water is closed to waterfowl. There is no approved acquisition boundary for the refuge so there are no inholdings. Figure 3 shows a general map of the refuge.

Its most extensive feature is the coastal marsh that includes the 8,785 acre Swanquarter National Wilderness Area. About 12,700 acres are low saltmarsh interspersed with potholes, creeks, and tidal drains. In higher areas, man-made canals, storm surges and sea-level rise have allowed saltwater intrusion to transform 1,600 acres of forested wetlands into brackish marsh dominated by sawgrass and sedges. The refuge is accessible only by boat except for the Bell Island area which is accessible by vehicle from US 264. Public use consists mostly of fishing and waterfowl hunting, wildlife viewing and photography at the Bell Island Pier and in the adjacent open waters.

North Carolina Wildlife Resources Commission's (NCWRC) Gull Rock Gamelands surround the Juniper Bay Compartment of Swanquarter NWR. This area is characterized by very remote pocosin vegetation mixed with hardwood swamps and salt marsh along the edge of Pamlico Sound. Perimeter roads and boat access from the sound shore provide limited access to the area with no established physical boundary between landowners. Therefore, fire management issues must be coordinated between the NCWRC, the North Carolina Division of Forests Resources (NCDFR), and the US Fish and Wildlife Service.

The refuge's CCP, completed in July 2008, is designed to guide the management of Swanquarter NWR for the next 15-years. Chapter II of the CCP (FWS 2008) includes a thorough description of the physical and biological environments on the refuge and the socioeconomic conditions of the surrounding area. Appendix I of the CCP is a list of refuge biota and includes the common and scientific names for species mentioned in this FMP.

Figure 3: Swanquarter National Wildlife Refuge – Current Lands

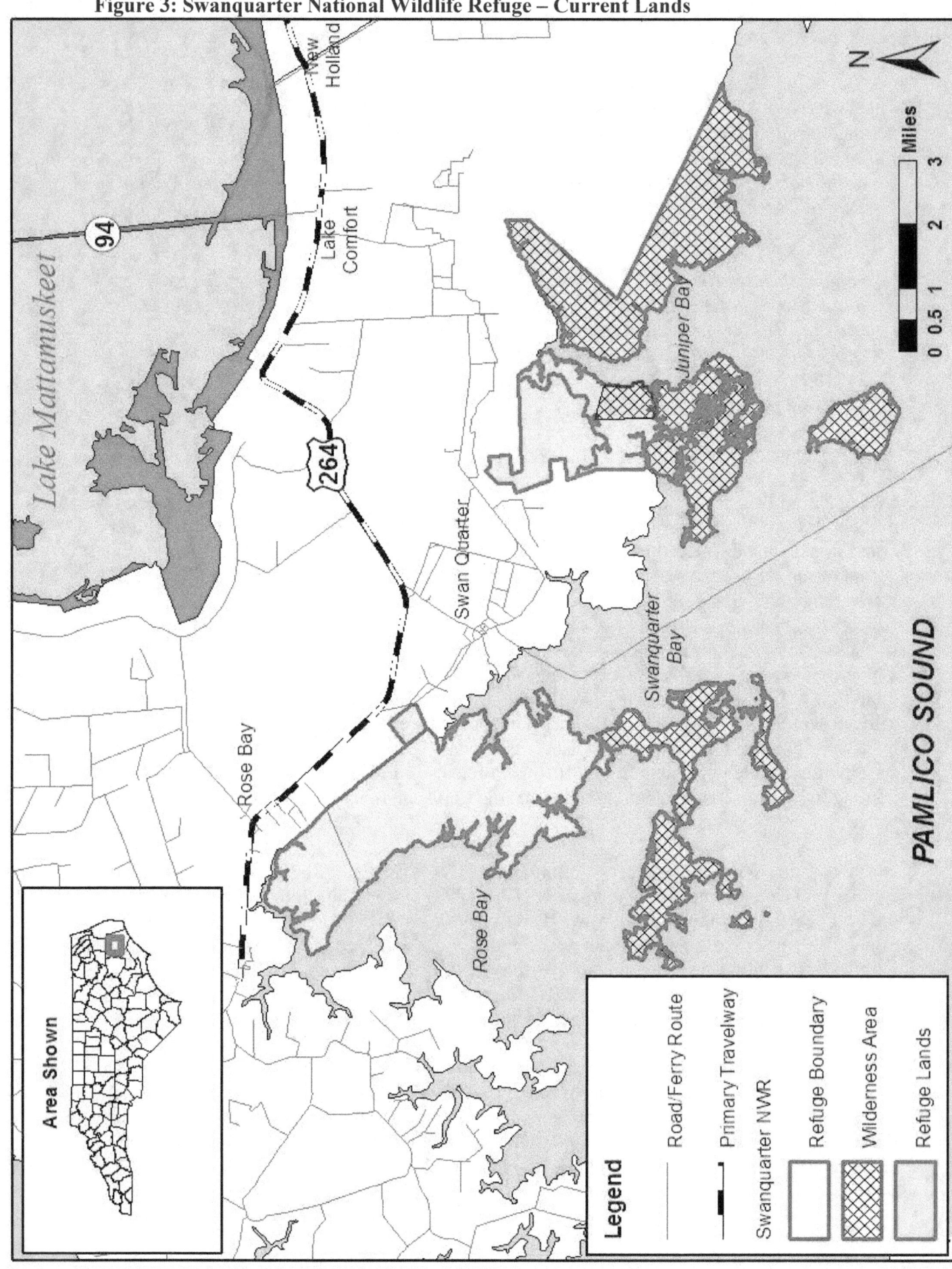

Lake Mattamuskeet

94

New Holland

Lake Comfort

264

Swan Quarter

Juniper Bay

Swanquarter Bay

Rose Bay

Rose Bay

PAMLICO SOUND

N

Miles
0 0.5 1   2   3

Area Shown

Legend

Road/Ferry Route	
Primary Travelway	
Swanquarter NWR	
Refuge Boundary	
Wilderness Area	
Refuge Lands	

6

The CCP (FWS 2008) established a vision for the refuge of which the following portions are pertinent to fire management on the refuge:

SwanquarterNWR functions as a vital part of National Wildlife Refuge System as an important wintering area for migratory birds, such as ducks, geese, and swans, on the Atlantic Flyway. The refuge maintains breeding habitat for a variety of migratory birds. The refuge protects and enhances a healthy brackish marsh ecosystem and an upland forest ecosystem, and maintains the natural and primitive character of the large wilderness area. The refuge provides habitat for threatened and endangered anaimals, particularly the red-cockcaded woodpecker, red wolf, and American alligator...The refuge staff works with partners and volunteers to achieve the refuge's goals. Essential scientific information is garnered through research conducted at Swanquarter NWR in cooperation with government agencies, non-governmental agencies, universities, and others

1.2.3. Cedar Island National Wildlife Refuge

Cedar Island NWR lies five miles east of the Atlantic Ocean, and 40 miles northeast of Beaufort, North Carolina (Figure 4). It is an estuarine barrier island located in Carteret County, at the mouth of the Pamlico Sound. The mainland terminus of NC Highway 12 ends on the north end of Cedar Island. At this point, the North Carolina Ferry System operates ferry boats that transport vehicles and passengers to and from Ocracoke Island. The United States Marine Corps (USMC), from Cherry Point Marine Corps Air Station in Havelock, NC, manages the 1,470 acre Atlantic Field that borders part of the refuge. The refuge works cooperatively with the USMC on fire management issues on the two properties. Approximately 2,405 acres of land within the Cedar Island NWR approved acquisition boundary (16,887 acres) are not owned by the Service.

The refuge is at the end of a peninsula at the south end of Pamlico Sound and consists of 14,462 acres -- approximately 11,000 acres of irregularly flooded saltmarsh, 3,395 acres of pocosin and woodlands, and 85 acres of land used for administrative purposes. The refuge's main feature is the extensive, relatively undisturbed coastal marsh. The refuge provides wintering habitat for thousands of ducks and nesting habitat for colonial waterbirds. Public use is primarily boating, fishing, waterfowl hunting and wildlife observation.

The refuge's CCP was completed in July 2006 to guide the management of Cedar Island NWR for the next 15-years. Chapter II of the CCP (FWS 2006) includes a thorough description of the physical and biological environments on the refuge and the socioeconomic conditions of the surrounding area. Appendix VI of the CCP is a list of refuge biota and includes the common and scientific names for species mentioned in this FMP.

The CCP (FWS 2006) established a vision for the refuge of which the following portions are pertinent to fire management on the refuge:

Cedar Island National Wildlife Refuge will play a vital role in the National Wildlife Refuge System. The refuge will establish a presence in the local community by partnering with agencies, developing research groups, and organizing friends groups

Figure 4: Cedar Island National Wildlife Refuge – Current Lands

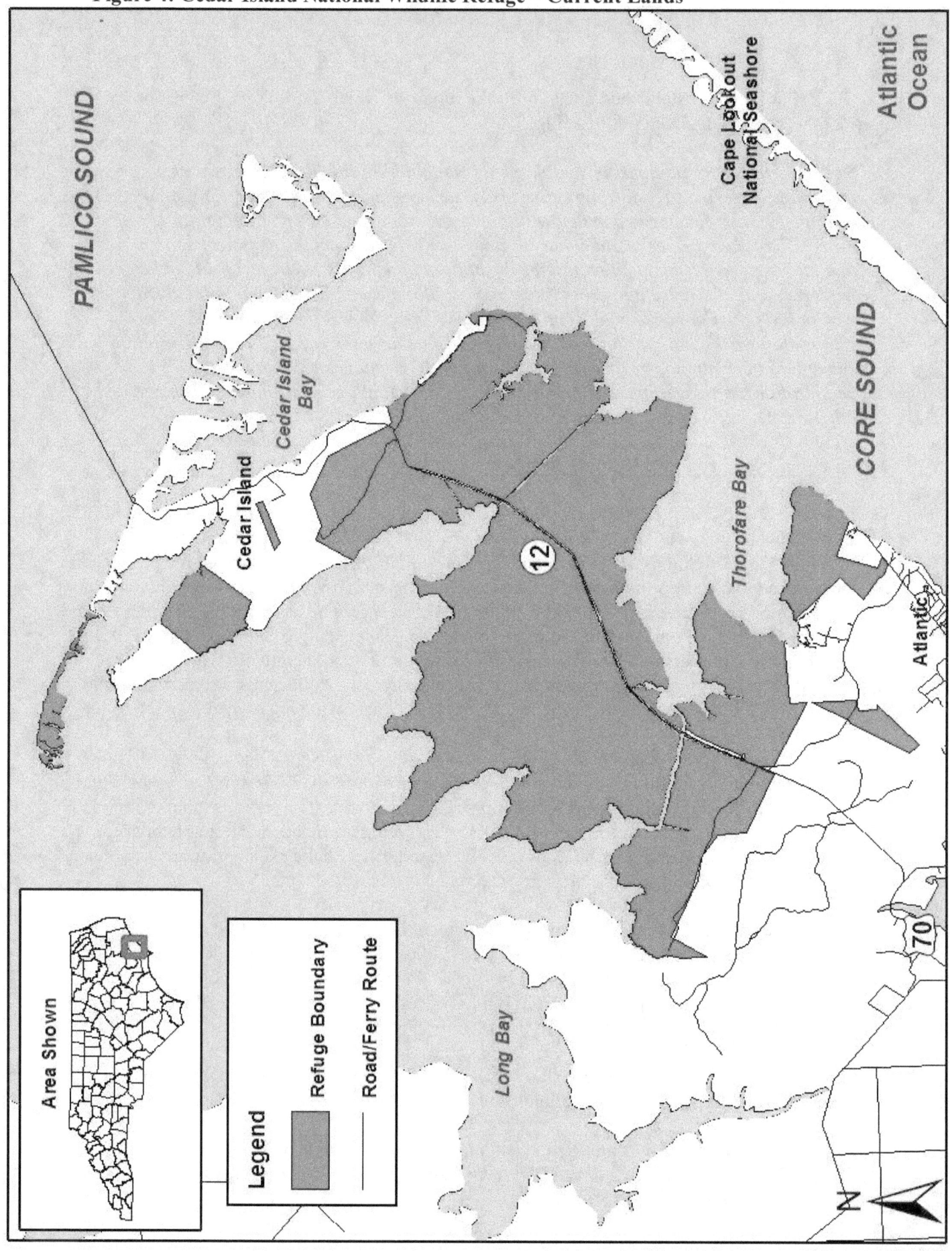

and volunteers. The refuge will conserve and manage fish and wildlife species, such as threatened and endangered species, species of management concern...Refuge staff and volunteers will protect the diverse habitats typical of the mid-Atlantic coastal ecosystem within which the refuge is situated, including coastal fringe forest, estuarine marsh, and longleaf pine savanna...Through active enhancement and management, the refuge will provide high quality, mid-Atlantic, coastal habitat for migratory birds and other priority species...Working with others, Cedar Island National Wildlife Refuge staff, partners, and volunteers will manage and protect the refuge's natural resources...

1.3. Significant Values to Protect

Special values emphasized for management common to the Mattamuskeet Complex are listed below.

- **Endangered Species:** The Mattamuskeet Complex provides habitat used by the American alligator, and there is potential habitat for the red-cockaded woodpecker (RCW). Mattamuskeet and Swanquarter NWRs are part of designated critical habitat for the endangered red wolf. The waters of the Pamlico Sound adjacent to Swanquarter and Cedar Island NWRs are used by the threatened loggerhead sea turtle.

- **Brackish and Freshwater Marshes:** These play a major role in the ecology of the estuarine systems of North Carolina, providing valuable wildlife habitats for a variety of species, including migratory waterfowl and fisheries. Marshes are fire adapted communities, interspersed between sounds, freshwater lakes and streams. Without disturbance (e.g. fire on a frequent cycle), this habitat will transition to domination by either one or two species of grasses, rushes, or shrubs.

- **Migratory Waterfowl and Shorebirds:** Habitat for these species is provided by croplands and moist soil impoundments at Mattamuskeet NWR and the brackish and freshwater marshes at Swanquarter and Cedar Island NWRs.

- **Other Wetland/Forest Types:** Most refuge forest lands are comprised of cypress swamps and/or various combinations of lowland pine, hardwood and pocosin habitats.

Maps showing the locations of the values to protect for each refuge are included in Appendix E3. Sections 3.2-3.4 list specific descriptions of values potentially at risk from wildland fires or fire suppression activities for the FMUs.

Mattamuskeet National Wildlife Refuge

Mattamuskeet NWR was acquired under authority of the National Industrial Recovery Act (48 Stat. 195) and established by Executive Order of Franklin D. Roosevelt on December 18, 1934, stating that the refuge is "A...reserved and set apart...as a refuge and breeding ground for birds and wild animals..." Its most significant feature is Lake Mattamuskeet (40,000 acres) - 16 miles long and five to six miles wide, but averaging only two feet deep. Lake water drains freely into Pamlico Sound via four man-made outlet canals. The concentrations of wintering waterfowl and the resulting hunting have given the lake national recognition. Waterfowl numbers exceed 100,000 each winter and include snow geese, Canada geese, tundra swans, and 22 duck species.

- FWS offices, visitor center, maintenance facility, weather station, and four residences in the headquarters area

- Listed as a Natural Heritage Area by the state of North Carolina

- Sayler's Ridge, a 73 acre tract of mature loblolly pine within the refuge, is a Research Natural Area included in a 153 acre National Natural Landmark

- Mattamuskeet Lodge, listed on the National Register of Historic Places

- U.S. Highway 264 and North Carolina Highway 94 run through or near refuge lands

Swanquarter National Wildlife Refuge

Swanquarter NWR was established in 1932 under the authority of The Migratory Bird Conservation Act of 1929 "as inviolate sanctuary or for any other management purpose, for migratory birds." The refuge includes 16,411 acres of irregularly-flooded brackish marsh and forested wetlands. A 27,000 acre Presidential Proclamation Area in adjacent Sound waters is closed to waterfowl hunting.

- Swanquarter Wilderness Area (8,785 acres)

- Bell Island Pier valued at over $500,000

- U.S. Highway 264 runs near refuge lands

Cedar Island National Wildlife Refuge

Cedar Island NWR was established in 1964 under the authority of The Migratory Bird Conservation Act of 1929 "as inviolate sanctuary or for any other management purpose, for migratory birds." As an estuarine barrier island, the refuge has similarities to barrier islands, but is the only such island in North Carolina to face inward towards Pamlico Sound. The extensive, relatively undisturbed coastal marsh is an important value on the refuge. It also harbors a small area of remnant long leaf pine savannah.

- Refuge office and maintenance compound, weather station, and a storage building

- North Carolina Highway 12 runs through the refuge

- Near the Cedar Island Ferry Station

2.0 Policy, Land Management Planning, and Partnerships

2.1. Implementation of Fire Policy

Appendix N contains a list of policy references that affect fire management on national wildlife refuges. Appendix III or Appendix C of each refuge's CCP contains another list of relevant legal mandates.

2.1.1. Federal Interagency Wildland Fire Policy

This FMP implements these guiding principles of federal wildland fire policy:

- Firefighter and public safety is the first priority in every fire management activity.

- The role of wildland fire as an essential ecological process and natural change agent has been incorporated into the planning process. Federal agency land and resource management plans set the objectives for the use and desired future condition of the various public lands.

- Fire management plans, programs, and activities support land and resource management plans and their implementation.

- Sound risk management is a foundation for all fire management activities. Risks and uncertainties relating to fire management activities must be understood, analyzed, communicated, and managed as they relate to the cost of either doing or not doing an activity.

- Fire management programs and activities are economically viable, based upon values to be protected, costs, and land and resource management objectives.

- Fire management plans and activities are based upon the best available science.

- Fire management plans and activities incorporate public health and environmental quality considerations.

- Federal, State, tribal, local, interagency, and international coordination and cooperation are essential.

- Standardization of policies and procedures among federal agencies is an ongoing objective.

2.1.2. National Fire Plan

This FMP meets the policy and direction in the National Fire Plan because it emphasizes the following primary goals of *A Collaborative Approach for Reducing Wildfire Risks to Communities and the Environment: 10-Year Comprehensive Strategy (10-Year Strategy)* and *Protecting People and Natural Resources: A Cohesive Fuels Treatment Strategy (Cohesive Fuels Treatment Strategy)*:

- improving fire prevention and suppression,

- reducing hazardous fuels,

- restoring fire-adapted ecosystems, and

- promoting community assistance.

2.1.3. Department of Interior (DOI) Fire Policy

This FMP incorporates and adheres to DOI policy stated in *620 DM 1* by giving full consideration to use of wildland fire as a natural process and as a tool during the land management planning process and by providing for the following:

- Wildland fires, whether on or adjacent to lands administered by the Department, which threaten life, improvements, or are determined to be a threat to natural and cultural resources or improvements under the Department's jurisdiction, will be considered emergencies and their suppression given priority over other Department programs.

- Bureaus shall cooperate in the development of interagency preparedness plans to ensure timely recognition of approaching critical wildland fire situations; to establish processes for analyzing situations and establishing priorities; and for implementing appropriate management responses to these situations.

- Bureaus will enforce rules and regulations concerning the unauthorized ignition of wildland fires, and aggressively pursue violations.

2.1.4. U.S. Fish and Wildlife Service (FWS) Fire Policy

This FMP addresses a full range of potential wildland fires and considers a full spectrum of tactical options (from monitoring to intensive management actions) for appropriate management response (AMR) to meet Fire Management Unit (FMU) objectives. It fully applies procedures and guidelines in the *FWS Fire Management Handbook* and the *Interagency Standards for Fire and Fire Aviation Operations (Redbook)* and affirms these key elements of FWS fire policy:

- Firefighter and public safety is the first priority of the wildland fire management program and all associated activities.

- Only trained and qualified leaders and agency administrators will be responsible for, and conduct, wildland fire management duties and operations.

- Trained and certified employees will participate in the wildland fire management program as the situation requires, and non-certified employees will provide needed support as necessary.

- Fire management planning, preparedness, wildfire and prescribed fire operations, other hazardous fuel operations, monitoring, and research will be conducted on an interagency basis with involvement by all partners to the extent practical.

- The responsible agency administrator has coordinated, reviewed, and approved this FMP to ensure consistency with approved land management plans, values to be protected, and natural and cultural resource management plans, and that it addresses public health issues related to smoke and air quality.

- Fire, as an ecological process, has been integrated into resource management plans and activities on a landscape scale, across agency boundaries, based upon the best available science.

- Wildland fire is used to meet identified resource management objectives and benefits when appropriate.

- Prescribed fire and other treatment types will be employed whenever they are the appropriate tool to reduce hazardous fuels and the associated risk of wildfire to human life, property, and cultural and natural resources and to manage our lands for habitats as mandated by statute, treaty, and other authorities.

- Appropriate management response will consider firefighter and public safety, cost effectiveness, values to protect, and natural and cultural resource objectives.

- Staff members will work with local cooperators and the public to prevent unauthorized ignition of wildfires on our lands.

2.1.5. Refuge-specific Fire Management Policy

The Southeast Region has a regional aviation requirement that all aviation users take the B-3 Refresher training every 2 years, rather than the national 3 year requirement.

2.2. Land / Resource Management Planning

This FMP will support the Service's initiative for Strategic Habitat Conservation (SHC), also known as Strategic Landscape Conservation, by fully supporting adaptive management and the use of science-based information to inform and develop fire management actions. SHC principles can be found at https://intranet.fws.gov/region4/SHC.

2.2.1. Land/Resource Planning Documents

The FMP is related to the goals and objectives for refuge management through the overall guidance provided by the *Mattamuskeet National Wildlife Refuge Comprehensive Conservation Plan* (FWS 2008), the *Swanquarter National Wildlife Refuge Comprehensive Conservation Plan* (FWS 2008), and the *Cedar Island National Wildlife Refuge Comprehensive Conservation Plan* (FWS 2006). Biological planning in the CCPs was in turn influenced by cooperative partnerships reflected in the North American Waterfowl Management Plan including the Atlantic Coast Joint Venture, Partners in Flight Plan, US Shorebird Conservation Plan, and the South Atlantic Migratory Bird Initiative.

Several CCP step-down management plans will affect the refuges' fire management program. As these plans are developed under the new CCPs, changes will be made to the FMP during its annual review if warranted to improve management efficiencies and resolve resource conflicts between plans. The following list includes those step-down plans that will most likely impact fire management operations on the refuges:

- Biological Inventory/Monitoring Plan
- Habitat Management Plan
- Moist Soil/Water Management Plan
- Marsh Management Plan
- Integrated Pest Management Plan
- Environmental Education Plan

The Southern Wildfire Risk Assessment (SWRA) is an interagency effort to characterize wildland fire risk to communities in the South. This GIS based tool will be utilized to generate planning maps, characterize communities at risk, guide development of Community Wildfire Protection Plans, and prioritize fuel treatment projects.

A Community Wildfire Protection Plan (CWPP) is an interagency, community developed plan to address wildland fire risk and actions on a community level. In the CWPP planning process, wildland-urban interface (WUI) areas can be designated for a community based on fire history and surrounding fuels. The CWPP also lays out actions for agency and community partners to carry out in order to address the community's wildland fire risk. Plans are designed to be reviewed and updated on a regular basis. CWPPs should be closely linked to the FMP in regards to Service involvement and accomplishment of FMP objectives. As CWPPs are developed for communities surrounding the Complex refuges, they will be added as an appendix to the.

Fire Program Analysis (FPA) is an interagency budgetary planning tool for fire management. The newest computer software for this planning tool will be utilized in Fiscal Year 2008 and 2009 to develop a national interagency fire budget for FY 2011 and each year thereafter. District 1 is part of the interagency North Carolina Coastal Fire Planning Unit (FPU). As part of the FPA process, the FPU will develop a series of preparedness, prevention, and fuels options which will shape the budget. As a strategic tool, the FPA budgetary planning process has the potential to influence selection of projects and positioning of fire resources across FWS Fire District 1.

2.2.2. Compliance with Regulatory Acts

National Environmental Policy Act (NEPA) compliance was accomplished by completion of an Environmental Assessment (EA) for the Fire Management Plan during the summer of 2009. After the analysis of the EA and any comments received during the public review period, the Service will decide whether to prepare an Environmental Impact Statement or issue a Finding of No Significant Impact (FONSI). A record of the decision will be maintained in the refuge files.

In conjunction with the 2009 EA, the refuge has requested an Intra-Agency Section 7 Consultation from Raleigh Ecological Services Office (ES). A copy will be included in the Appendix of the EA.

The FMP must comply with Section 118 of the Clean Air Act. A geographic area that meets or does better than the primary standards for air pollutants is called an attainment area; areas that do not meet the primary standards for each pollutant are called non-attainment areas. Mattamuskeet and Swanquarter NWRs are located in Hyde County and Cedar Island NWR is located in Carteret County. Since these counties have currently been designated by the EPA as attainment areas for all criteria pollutants, a Clean Air Act Conformity determination is not necessary. Consideration of air quality is further discussed in Section 4.2.1.5 under smoke management for prescribed burning.

All FMP actions comply with Section 106 of the 1966 National Historic Preservation Act and Archeological Resources Protection Act of 1979. All known archeological and cultural resources are identified in Section 3 under the appropriate FMU values to protect. Should any other potential historical or cultural resources be discovered during fire operations, personnel will notify refuge management and take appropriate steps to safeguard the site and prevent further disturbance. Regional Archaeologist Richard Kanaski at Savannah Coastal Refuges is our cultural resources expert should issues on cultural resources arise.

Permits for any activities covered by the Section 404 permitting process, such as non-emergency firelines, will be submitted as required to the U.S. Army Corps of Engineers (Corps). Emergency firelines must be coordinated with the Corps as soon as practical. Plowed firelines in marshes are prohibited when other viable fireline options or alternative strategies are available. For compliance with the Federal Coastal Zone Management Act of 1972, a federal Consistency Determination has been prepared and will be submitted to the North Carolina Division of Coastal Management for concurrence. The Consistency Determination will be maintained in the files at the Complex headquarters.

Individual projects may need separate, individual clearance to comply with all regulatory acts and will be reviewed on a project basis.

2.3. Fire Management Partnerships

The U.S. Fish and Wildlife Service in the Southeast Region, Fire Management District 1 places development of cooperative relations as an extremely high priority. Sharing resources during wildfires is the primary advantage of cooperative relationships. Due to the hazardous fuels, poor soil trafficability, remoteness, and poor visibility on Refuge and adjoining Department of Defense, state, and private lands, no one agency has the capability to be self-sufficient for initial or extended attack. The FWS in northeastern North Carolina will always depend on cooperators, primarily the North Carolina Division of Forest Resources (NCDFR), for assistance.

Cooperative ties between agencies are also becoming more important for prescribed burning, other non-fire fuel treatments, and fire prevention and outreach projects. As prescribed burning activities increase within the agencies in northeastern North Carolina, cooperative assistance will play a greater role in helping these agencies carry out their programs. District fire management and Refuge staff will continue to cooperate and seek partnerships with nearby agencies and communities to increase the efficiency, productivity, and safety of all fire management activities on the Complex.

2.3.1. Internal Partnerships

The Mattamuskeet Complex and six other national wildlife refuges that comprise the North Carolina Coastal Plain Refuge Complex, are involved in a fire management partnership and together these refuges form the FWS Southeast Region Fire District 1. District fire personnel that work on fire management issues across the District include a District Fire Management Officer (DFMO), Prescribed Fire Specialist, Wildland-Urban Interface Specialist, and a Fire Program Technician. These positions are all based at Alligator River NWR. An Assistant District FMO is based at Pocosin Lakes NWR. Operational fire resources from across the District work together on all the district refuges to implement fire management activities.

2.3.2. External Partnerships

The U.S. Fish and Wildlife Service is part of an interagency agreement for wildland fire management response in North Carolina. The *Master Cooperative Wildland Fire Management and Stafford Act Response Agreement* (Master Agreement) is between the Service's Southeast and Northeast Regions, National Park Service (NPS), Bureau of Indian Affairs, U.S. Forest Service (USFS), and the NCDFR for wildland fire management in North Carolina. An Annual Operations Plan (AOP) sets forth the operational guidelines of this agreement within District 1 and includes the NPS, NCDFR, and Great Dismal Swamp NWR in the Northeast Region. In the future other state and local AOPs may be developed as step down plans of the wider interagency agreement. The AOP is included in Appendix A.

The Forestry Division employed by USMC at Cherry Point Marine Corps Air Station (MCAS) is a primary cooperator, especially at Cedar Island NWR. A Memorandum of Understanding (MOU) for fire management between the MCAS and Cedar Island NWR covers both wildfire suppression and prescribed burning. The Nature Conservancy (TNC) also cooperates in interagency fire operations at Cedar Island NWR and other refuges under a FWS Southeast Region agreement. Many of the prescribed burns conducted during the past 10 years at Cedar Island NWR have relied on resources from the USMC and TNC.

Following the closest resource concept, the NCDFR is a primary cooperator, especially at Cedar Island NWR where the closest FWS fire resources are 3 or more hours away. At Cedar Island NWR, the NCDFR will make an initial response to wildfires while simultaneously informing the Service (Appendix A). The Service has also developed cooperative relations with several Volunteer Fire Departments (VFD) through grant agreements with the Rural Fire Assistance Program. Over the next five years, the District plans to strengthen these ties through cooperative agreements with AOPs and development of CWPPs.

The Mattamuskeet Complex is also involved in a partnership for federal fire budget planning called Fire Program Analysis (FPA). The country was divided into Fire Planning Units (FPU), and the agencies within an FPU are working together to develop an interagency fire budget. The Complex is part of the North Carolina Coast FPU which includes all the national wildlife refuges in District 1, the Croatan National Forest, Cape Hatteras National Seashore, and Cape Lookout National Seashore.

To facilitate prescribed burning, the Mattamuskeet Complex or District has entered into several Memoranda of Understanding with private landowners or agencies. These are covered in Section 3 under the affected Fire Management Unit.

A Draft FMP and EA will be made available for public comment and review for 30 days. Relevant comments and concerns received during the review period will be considered for incorporation into the Final FMP. Regional Service fire staff and local fire management cooperators will be consulted for input during the public review period. A complete list of contacts is given in the EA.

3.0 Fire Management Units

For the purpose of fire management each refuge in the Mattamuskeet Complex is a Fire Management Unit (FMU). FMUs are divided into Fire Compartments in which wildfires or prescribed fires can be contained within physical bounds, given favorable weather and fireline improvement. Fire Compartments are further broken down into Burn Units. Table 2 lists the number of compartments and burn units in each FMU.

Table 2: Fire Management Units

FMU Name	# of Compartments	# of Burn Units	Total Acres	Burnable Acres
Mattamuskeet NWR	4	33	50,180	10,155
Swanquarter NWR	5	14	16,411	16,400
Cedar Island NWR	7	31	14,480	14,395

Under the Master Agreement, a mutual threat zone was defined as lands within 1/2 mile of refuge property where there is potential for fires to impact Service lands. Under FPA, 1 mile mutual threat zones were formally delineated as FMUs, but they are not under this FMP. The Service will respond to fires in the mutual threat zone per the Master Agreement and AOP. Table 3 lists the FMUs as delineated in FPA.

Table 3: Fire Management Units in FPA

Fire Management Units	Acres*
Mattamuskeet	49,720
Mattamuskeet Threat	10,530
Swanquarter	15,910
Swanquarter Threat	11,260
Cedar Island	14,280
Cedar Island Threat	9,131

* GIS generated acres.

3.1. Area Wide Management Considerations

3.1.1. Management Goals, Objectives and Constraints in CCPs

The refuges' CCPs have broad refuge management goals related to fish and wildlife populations, habitat, public use, resource protection, and administration with more specific objectives and strategies identified under each broad goal. The following fire management goals for Mattamuskeet, Swanquarter, and Cedar Island NWRs reflect the goals and objectives as identified in the CCPs. More specific fire management objectives are listed by Fire Management Unit in Sections 3.2 to 3.4.

1. Manage wildland fires on refuge lands to minimize risks to firefighter and public safety.

2. Develop and implement a process to ensure the collection, analysis and application of high quality fire management information needed for sound management decisions. Adaptively manage fuel treatments and wildfire response by developing and implementing a fire effects monitoring plan and effective use of After Action Reviews.

3. Consider impacts to the integrity of wetlands during planning and implementation of all fire management activities. The effects of climate change and sea-level rise on these ecosystems will also be considered in fire management.

4. Use fire to accomplish resource management objectives when and where possible, to enhance existing habitat for migratory birds and to enhance existing and potential habitat for specific endangered species.

5. Continuously develop and manage a Refuge fire organization consisting of firefighters, equipment operators, and other specialists capable of safely and effectively addressing fire management needs for Mattamuskeet, Swanquarter, and Cedar Island NWRs as well as integrating with staff from other refuges and the hatchery to meet fire management needs on the District.

6. Develop cooperative relations with neighboring fire management districts, refuges, cooperators and interagency partners to facilitate overall fire management missions within multiple jurisdictions in northeastern North Carolina and the State as a whole.

7. Develop a High Reliability Organization in which the safety and well-being of firefighters and the public are always paramount above all other objectives within the refuges and district fire management programs.

8. Conduct fuel treatments with the highest professional and technical standards to achieve resource management objectives, hazardous fuel reduction, and community protection.

9. Support the development and implementation of other CCP step-down plans that would affect fire management on the refuges, such as plans for habitat management, invasive species, and endangered species.

10. Educate the public regarding the use of fire as a habitat management, resource protection, and community protection tool.

3.1.2. Management Goals, Objectives and Constraints from other sources

The following goals, objectives and constraints are taken from various policy or guidance documents that affect fire management on national wildlife refuges (see Appendix N).

- **Fire Management Goals and Objectives**

1. Respond to every wildfire on or threatening our lands with an Appropriate Management Response, taking into consideration public and firefighter safety, impacts to natural resources, and cost effectiveness.

2. Use wildland fire to protect, maintain and enhance resources and, as nearly as possible, be allowed to function in its natural ecological role. This can be achieved through the use of

planned and unplanned ignitions that follow specific prescriptions contained in operational plans.

3. The range of appropriate management responses to wildfires may include direct or indirect attack strategies or surveillance and monitoring to ensure fire spread will be limited to a designated area.

4. Confine wildland fire to refuge lands where possible. Where feasible and needed to meet refuge goals and objectives, develop agreements to allow fire activity on private or other agency lands.

5. Wildfires in wilderness or candidate wilderness areas will receive an appropriate management response that includes consideration of wilderness values and completion of a minimum tool analysis in support of the AMR.

6. Consider smoke management to the extent possible when developing tactics to meet an AMR.

7. When specifically addressed in approved FMPs, we can use naturally ignited wildland fires to accomplish resource management objectives.

8. Take necessary measures to protect visibility and safety for motorists along highways and major roads during wildfires or prescribed fire treatments.

- **Fire Management Constraints**

1. Aerial or ground application of fire retardants, foams, and water enhancers should be avoided within 300 feet of waterways unless life or property is threatened and their use can reasonably be expected to alleviate the threat. Other exceptions can be found in Chapter 12 of the *Redbook*.

2. Use of retardant, foam, and aircraft in wilderness, RNA, and other special areas will require approval from the Refuge Manager.

3. The Refuge Manager is the decision authority for equipment use in wilderness areas on Swanquarter NWR and Research Natural Areas (RNA) on Mattamuskeet NWR. Use of heavy equipment in wilderness areas will require Regional Office concurrence.

4. Agency firefighters will not take direct suppression actions on structure, vehicle, or landfill fires, but limit firefighting efforts to areas where the fire has spread onto agency protected lands.

5. Smoke management laws, smoke dispersion patterns, and considerations for military operations narrow available burn windows and can constrain prescribed burning activities on the refuges.

- **Cost Effectiveness**

Maximizing the cost effectiveness of any fire operation is the responsibility of all involved, including those that authorize, direct, or implement these operations. Cost effectiveness is the most economical use of the resources necessary to accomplish project/incident objectives. Accomplishing these objectives safely and efficiently will not be sacrificed for the sole purpose of "cost savings." Care will be taken to ensure that expenditures are commensurate with values to be protected. Many factors outside of the biophysical environment may influence spending decisions, including those of the social, political, and economic realms. Hazardous fuels projects will be planned for the most economical, effective, and safe treatment that is commensurate with the values to protect. The Wildland Fire Decision Support System (WFDSS) or other required wildfire decision support tool will be used for analysis of integrated risk and cost management.

3.1.3. Common Characteristics of the Fire Management Units

The lands in the Mattamuskeet Complex are all relatively flat, low-lying, and near sea level. Because of the proximity of large bodies of relatively warm water, combined with flat topography and low elevations, the climate of all three refuges is similar. Summers are hot and humid with temperatures occasionally climbing above 95 degrees Fahrenheit (F). Winters are moderately cool, with temperatures seldom falling below 20°F. On rare occasions portions of Lake Mattamuskeet freeze, but never for a long period. Marsh areas frequently freeze in January and February. Mean summer high temperatures range from of 77 to 83°F at Mattamuskeet and Cedar Island NWRs. Mean winter low temperature is 41°F. The mean annual precipitation is 50 to 53 inches, with periods of heavy rainfall from July through September. Snowfall is rare and seldom exceeds 2 inches. Evapo-transpiration losses tend to be more constant from year to year than rainfall. During the months of April, May and June, evapo-transpiration exceeds rainfall.

Fire weather is difficult to predict because the proximity of the Mattamuskeet Complex to the coast creates localized weather conditions. The large bodies of water, such as the Atlantic Ocean, Pamlico Sound, and Lake Mattamuskeet can cause local winds that can change suddenly in speed and direction. The Outer Banks is considered one of the windiest locations on the East Coast. Strong low and high pressure systems can create very tight pressure gradients with strong winds.

The probable fire regimes in the coastal plain of eastern North Carolina are documented (Frost 1986, 1995) and were a frequent and a driving-force in shaping the ecosystem found there. It is also known that Native Americans used fire to manipulate their environment in eastern North Carolina. In addition, coastal storms (e.g. tropical storms, hurricanes, and northeasters) are the primary natural disturbance agents in the area that interact with fire and affect the vegetative community. This region has been historically driven by natural disturbance. A detailed wildfire history from 1966 to present is included in Appendix P.

Most native vegetation is either fire dependent or fire adapted with characteristic rapid regeneration. A direct loss of ground cover and understory vegetation often results from wildfire, but seldom results in permanent damage to an ecosystem. Economic losses from wildfire can be large as evidenced in the 1985 wildfire that burned from Open Ground Farms to the north end of Cedar Island destroying stands of mature and immature longleaf and loblolly pine. Long-term damage to the ecosystem was minimal because of the regeneration of most vegetation types. The most wildfire damage results when areas containing organic soils or thick duff and litter burn too deeply or too hot and kill tree roots which leads to tree mortality. The crowns of all pine species are susceptible to needle scorch during intense fires, but scorching seldom results in heavy tree mortality.

Following a wildfire, sprouting increases for many plant species such as red maple, wax myrtle, redbay, American holly, choke cherry, persimmon, American elm, wild grape, Virginia creeper, and rattan. This growth benefits wildlife species such as white-tailed deer, northern bobwhite quail, black bear, and many songbirds.

In freshwater marshes, wildfire consumes cattail, phragmites, red maple, buttonbush, bald cypress, groundsel and wax myrtle. Saltmarsh fuels include needlerush, saltmarsh cordgrass, and groundsel bush. Dead grasses and live and dead brush are reduced to ash, providing for a more productive and diverse plant community. In addition, fire can expose the seeds of marsh plants making them more available to migratory birds.

Table 4:Vegetation, Fuel Models, and Fire Behavior

Refuge	Vegetative Cover	Acres	Fuel Models	Fire Behavior Expected
Mattamuskeet	Marsh/impoundments	6,425	3 Tall Grass	Intense, with high spread rates. Fire can cross water in tips of grass.
Swanquarter	Saltmarsh	11,000		
Cedar Island		11,000		
Mattamuskeet	Shrub Pocosin		4 Chaparral, 6 Dormant Brush	Potential erratic fire behavior in model 4. Moderate in 6.
Swanquarter				
Cedar Island		500		
Mattamuskeet	Forest and woodlands	2,430	7 Southern Rough, 8/ 9 Forest Litter	Intense, flammable live fuels in 7. Moderate or low behavior in 8 and 9.
Swanquarter		3,395		
Cedar Island		2,441		

Appropriate Management Response is thoroughly covered in Section 4.1 and can include a range of strategic options such as monitoring, indirect attack, direct attack, and point protection. At times, more than one or perhaps all these strategic responses may be required in combination to meet the needs for an AMR. Sections 3.2 – 3.4 contain a description of AMRs for each refuge. The listed AMRs are not to be viewed as the only appropriate actions in an FMU, but the most likely responses that would be taken. Each wildland fire is unique with its own set of weather, fire behavior, resource, and event variables that must be taken into consideration by the Incident Commander (IC) when choosing an AMR.

The refuges share several safety considerations. Poison ivy, venomous snakes, ticks, mosquitoes, and biting flies can pose a hazard to firefighters at almost any time of the year. Getting wet during fire management operations is a definite possibility and has the potential to lead to hypothermia. During the summer, high temperatures and humidity can lead to dangerous heat indices that can cause heat exhaustion or lead to dehydration. Wet, soft organic soils can contribute to vehicles and equipment getting stuck and then entrapped by advancing fire. The difficulty of seeing the fire from the ground in heavy concentrations of shrub and timber fuels further compounds the dangers, especially when equipment operators cannot see each other or where they are going in relation to the fire. The only way to mitigate this situation in direct attack scenarios is to have a trained aerial observer overhead when attacking a fire with equipment AND the tractor plow strike team must carry the black line with them by burning out their plow line. The safest method of fighting fire in most instances is with an indirect attack suppression strategy using a series of pre-prepared firebreaks or some improvised on scene. This works very well at Cedar Island and Swanquarter NWRs where forest values are primarily related to wildlife habitat, not commercial timber.

The greatest threat to public safety relates to smoke-reduced visibility on the highways that are in or adjacent to the refuges. The second greatest concern is for wildfires associated with high wind events that push a wildfire through hazardous fuels and into the communities adjacent to refuge lands. Management emphasis during wildfires needs to focus on mitigating any resulting impacts.

3.2. Fire Management Unit 1 – Mattamuskeet NWR

Table 5: 10-Year Average by Fiscal Year (1999-2008) for Wildland Fire Management Activities on Mattamuskeet NWR

Type	Number	Acres
Wildfires	0.4	0.3
Prescribed Burns	1.7	209.6
Non-Fire Projects	1.1	12.6

3.2.1 Mattamuskeet FMU Characteristics

The refuge is 50,180 acres (10,155 burnable acres) in and surrounding Lake Mattamuskeet. The lower land is only slightly higher than the lake level. Islands in the lake are often flooded by wind-driven tides or high water. Spoil areas are one to six feet above sea level. The soils range from fine sands to peaty soils. Sandy soil predominates on the uplands, particularly around the rim of the lake. Low lying areas are typically peaty silt overlying a sandy subsoil.

The vegetation is seasonally-flooded freshwater marsh, impoundments, and cropland (FM 3) and forest and woodlands (FM 7, 8, 9). Locally developed fuel model maps are shown in Figure 5. Since the establishment of Mattamuskeet NWR in the 1934, prescribed fires have been used to manage the habitat. The refuge is divided into fire Compartments and Burn Units which are delineated on Figure 10 (see Section 4.2). The refuge has had only a few historic natural or human-caused wildfires that have been generally controlled with hand tools and natural firebreaks. However, several of those fires have easily crossed from private lands onto the refuge. This potential to cross ownership lines has been a primary consideration in planning recent mechanical fuel treatments.

Figure 5: Mattamuskeet National Wildlife Refuge – Fuel Models

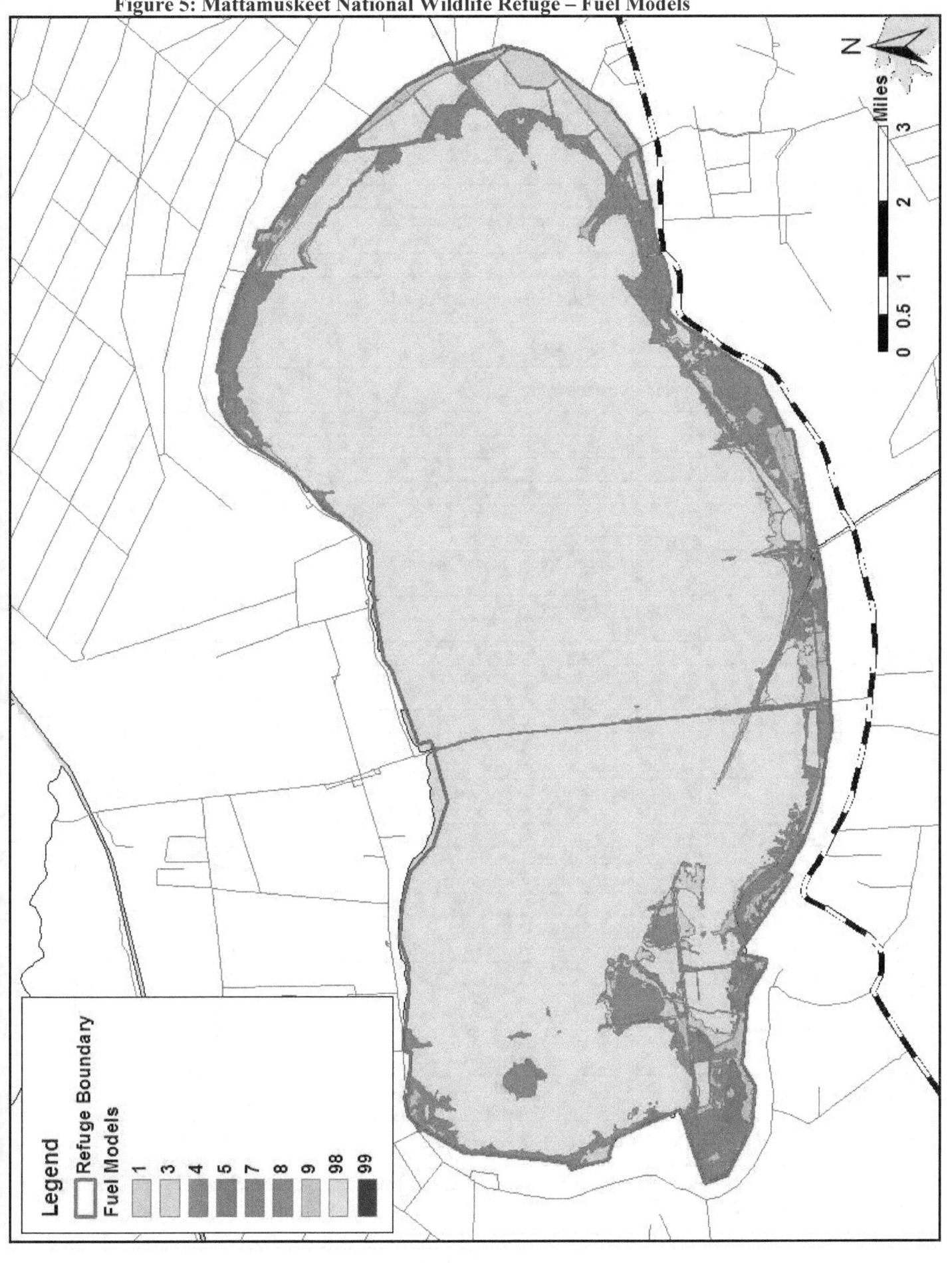

Legend

Refuge Boundary

Fuel Models
1
3
4
5
7
8
9
98
99

N

0 0.5 1 2 3
Miles

3.2.2. Mattatmuskett FMU Values to Protect

Values to Protect	Description	Risk
Threatened & Endangered Species		
red wolf	critical habitat	endangered species
Air Quality		
Hyde County communities and transportation corridors	potential smoke impacts to air quality and visibility	life, human health, socio-economic impacts
WUI		
Lake Comfort	state recognized Community At Risk (CAR)	life, property, human health, socio-economic impacts
Lake Landing	state recognized CAR	life, property, human health, socio-economic impacts
New Holland	state recognized CAR	life, property, human health, socio-economic impacts
Cultural Resources		
Mattamuskeet Lodge	National Register of Historic Places	socio-economic impacts
Natural Resources		
key wildlife habitat	important for wintering waterfowl	natural, wildlife
Special Designations		
SNHA	significant natural heritage area	natural, wildlife
Sayler's Ridge NRA	state natural research area and National Natural Landmark	wilderness attributes
Mattamuskeet Islands	proposed wilderness area	wilderness attributes
Recreation		
hunting	public hunting available in FMU	life, human health, recreation
fishing	public fishing in navigable waterways and 2 wood fishing piers along NC 94	life, human health, recreation, infrastructure
visitor outdoor displays	kiosk, signs	life, human health, recreation
public boat ramps	boat ramp at Rose Bay Canal & concrete ramp, wooden dock and parking area at Central Canal	life, property, human health, recreation
wildlife observation	wood boardwalk on New Holland Trail & East Main Drive, wood observation deck on NC 94	life, human health, recreation, infrastructure
Right-of-ways		
utility right-of-way	utility poles and telephone boxes along US Hwy 264 and buried lines along NC 94	utilities
Infrastructure		
US Highway 264	major transportation corridor	highway safety
NC Highway 94	major transportation corridor	highway safety
Refuge property		
pumping stations	At impoundments MI-2,4, 5/6, 7,8,9,10 &11, FA-1 and FA-2	government property
water control structures	At impoundments MI-1, 3, 5, 6, 8, 10 & 11 and major canals throughout refuge	government property
Complex headquarters	offices, equipment housing, fire cache, garage, maintenance facilities	government facilities
employee residences	4 refuge houses in headquarters area	life, government facility, private property
weather station	remote access weather station (RAWS)	government property
air quality monitor	wood building on south levee of MI-4	government property

3.2.3. Mattamuskeet FMU Management Guidance

- **AMR**

The table below gives examples of potential AMRs for the Mattamuskeet FMU. Specific AMR objectives for this FMU include:

1. Protect communities and private structures through cooperation with the NCDFR and local VFDs.

2. Confine fires within the roads circling Lake Mattamuskeet (US 264, Turnpike Road, Piney Woods Road, and North Lake Road).

3. Consider wilderness values and Minimum Impact Suppression Tactics (MIST) in selection of AMR for fires occurring in the Slayer's Ridge RNA and on the islands in Lake Mattamuskeet.

FMU 1 Appropriate Management Response

Potential situations	Potential strategies	Potential tactics
Fire burning in accessible area near a road or water access, small enough to conduct successful expedient direct attack.	Direct attack	Use engines to suppress fires near roads, portable pumps and boats to suppress fires with water access. Marshmasters and tractors may be used if deemed safe and expedient to suppress the fire.
Fire threatens to escape the boundary of a compartment or threatens values within.	Point protection (used in conjunction with direct or indirect attack as needed.)	Use engines and tractors as needed to protect values or critical holding lines. Pumps and irrigations systems may be set up to aid in protection when time is available. Use aerially applied water, foam or retardant if warranted and approved.
Fire occurs or escapes into impoundments or one of the extremely boggy woodland sections.	Indirect attack.	Use engines and tractors to hold or burn out critical control lines as needed. Monitor or burn out remainder of fuels in compartment as needed to contain the fire.

- **Hazardous Fuels**

The primary hazardous fuel consideration in this FMU is to promote ecosystem health through regular burning that prevents the build-up of hazardous fuels. Fuel treatments will use a variety of methods that may include maintenance of roads and firebreaks, control of invasive species, and community fuel reduction projects. Specific fuel treatment objectives for Mattamuskeet FMU include;

1. Apply prescribed fire as appropriate to managed impoundments and emergent lakeshore vegetation to promote early-successional wetland plants (i.e. annuals) to benefit migratory birds and other wildlife.

2. Conducted prescribed burns in designated upland burn units, striving for a 3-5 year fire return interval.

3. Conducted prescribed burns in farm fields striving for a 3-5 year fire return interval to control woody fuels.

4. Construct a fuelbreak along the refuge boundary where appropriate to decrease the likelihood of fire crossing off of or onto the refuge for the protection of private lands, refuge resources, and WUI areas.

5. Maintain 132 acres of roads, firebreaks, and dikes annually or as needed in this FMU in preparation for wildfire control, prescribed burn treatments, road maintenance, and control of woody plants.

6. Over the next 5 years, investigate the potential to implement fuel treatments in the Slayer's Ridge RNA, including biological and fuel management considerations.

3.2.4. Mattamuskeet FMU Safety Considerations

Most of the FMU is open to the public. Mattamuskeet NWR has several lottery hunts for waterfowl and deer from September through January. The lake is open to the public and there are two public boat ramps on the refuge.

NC 94 is a paved two-lane highway that runs north-south across Lake Mattamuskeet. Although the highway has relatively wide shoulders across the lake, there are often private vehicles parked alongside the highway from people fishing or bird watching. US 264 is a major transportation corridor in the county and is a paved, two-lane road with narrow shoulders. The road is very curvy and is often used by wide farm tractors that can make passing difficult and dangerous. Neither road receives heavy traffic, but vehicle traffic is constant enough to be a concern for smoke impacts and firefighter safety.

3.3. Fire Management Unit 2 – Swanquarter NWR

Table 6: 10-Year Average by Fiscal Year (1999-2008) for Wildland Fire Management Activities on Swanquarter NWR

Type	Number	Acres
Wildfires	0.4	151.3
Prescribed Burns	1.8	1669.6
Non-Fire Projects	0.1	0.7

3.3.1. Swanquarter FMU Characteristics

Swanquarter NWR is 16,411 acres (16,400 burnable acres) bordering Pamlico Sound with the majority of the refuge inaccessible by ground. The vegetation is predominantly irregularly-flooded saltwater marsh (FM 3), shrub pocosin (FM 4, 6), and forest and woodlands (FM 7, 8, 9). Locally developed fuel model maps are shown in Figure 6. The saltmarsh soils are characterized by a layer of root moss about one foot in depth over a peat layer of eight feet or more which overlies a sandy blue clay mineral base. Organic soils impede fire operations when water-saturated, making traverse with equipment extremely difficult. During droughts, with low soil moisture and deep water tables, heavy equipment may be able to operate; however, conditions can lead to long duration fires.

The refuge is divided into fire Compartments and Burn Units which are delineated on Figure 11 (see Section 4.2). The refuge's first prescribed fire was conducted in the Bell Island Compartment (Compartment 1) in 1991 (690 acres). Since this time, all the marsh, pine stands and much of the swamp fuels in the Bell Island Compartment have been burned for three or four times. The areas on the west side of Juniper Bay have been treated in the past with prescribed burning. These areas include Marsh Island (Compartment 3), the Judith Islands (Compartment 2) and Great Island (Compartment 4). However, due to questions regarding the management of wilderness values in these compartments, prescribed burning has been put on hold pending further assessment. The land area east of Juniper Bay along with the adjacent Gull Rock Gamelands have never been prescribed burned, but there have been discussions with the NCWRC on developing burn plans in the future. The District has a MOU with the NCWRC for each agency to assist the other in conducting prescribed burns on adjacent lands. The Gull Rock Gamelands abut the east side of the refuge in Compartment 5, and may be burned in conjunction with Burn Unit 2.5.1.

The refuge does not have an extensive fire history. Seventeen wildfires have occurred on or threatened Swanquarter NWR since 1972. The fires burned from one acre to 1500 acres in size. Known fire causes include: lightning, smoldering snags from previous fires, car fire, an airplane crash, boating flare and converted prescribed burn.

Figure 6: Swanquarter National Wildlife Refuge – Fuel Models

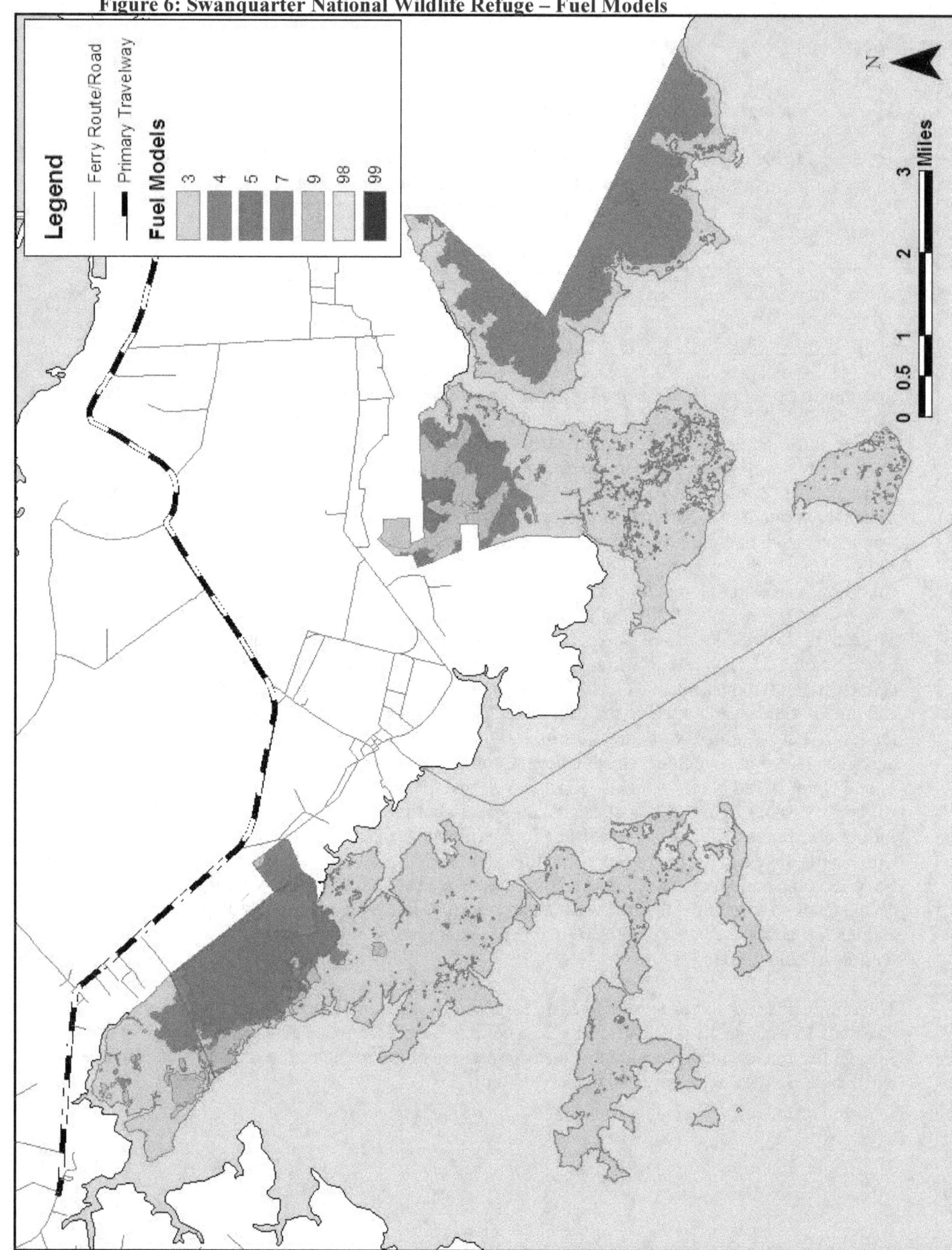

3.2.2. Swanquarter FMU Values to Protect

Values to Protect	Description	Risk
Threatened & Endangered Species		
red wolf	critical habitat	endangered species
Air Quality		
Class I Airshed	potential smoke impacts to air quality and visibility may impact the visitor experience	air quality, recreation
Hyde County communities and transportation corridors	potential smoke impacts to air quality and visibility	life, human health, socio-economic impacts
WUI		
Swan Quarter	state recognized Community At Risk (CAR)	life, property, human health, socio-economic impacts
Rose Bay	state recognized CAR	life, property, human health, socio-economic impacts
Natural Resources		
Wetlands	sensitive organic soils and estuarine values	natural, water quality
Special Designations		
SNHA	significant natural heritage area	natural, wildlife
Swanquarter Wilderness	wilderness area	wilderness attributes
Recreation		
hunting	public hunting available in FMU	life, human health, recreation
fishing	public fishing from pier and adjacent waterways	life, human health, recreation
Bell Island Pier	popular wooden fishing pier and one portable restroom	public use, refuge infrastructure
Right-of-ways		
utility right-of-way	utility poles and telephone boxes along US Hwy 264	utilities
Infrastructure		
US Highway 264	major transportation corridor	highway safety
Refuge property		
duck boxes	scattered wood duck boxes	government property

3.3.3. Swanquarter FMU Management Guidance

- **AMR**

The table below gives examples of potential AMRs for the Swanquarter FMU. Specific AMR objectives for this FMU include:

1. Protect communities and private property values through cooperation with the NCDFR and local VFDs.

2. Confine fires to refuge lands where possible and keep fire south of US 264.

3. Consider wilderness values and MIST in selection of AMR for fires occurring in the wilderness areas.

4. Manage wildfires to achieve resource and hazardous fuels benefits wherever and

whenever appropriate based on values at risk, potential impacts and potential costs.

5. Work together with the NCWRC to develop AMR strategies that allow the use of wildland fire to function in its natural ecological role within the Juniper Bay Compartment and Gull Rock Gamelands.

FMU 2 Appropriate Management Response

Potential situations	Potential strategies	Potential tactics
Fire burning in accessible area near a road or water access, small enough to conduct direct attack.	Direct attack	Use engines to suppress fires near roads, portable pumps and boats to suppress fires with water access. Marshmasters and tractors may be used if deemed safe and expedient to suppress the fire.
Fire occurs or escapes into one of the interior sections of compartments.	Indirect attack.	Use engines and tractors to hold or burn in critical control lines as needed. Monitor or burn out remainder of compartment as needed.
Fire occurs or escapes into one of the interior sections of compartments.	Monitor the fire, establishing Management Action Points with trigger points and pre-determined response.	Monitor with aircraft. Use aerially applied retardant, or water, engines and tractors as holding resources as needed to keep the fire contained within the compartment.
Fire threatens to escape the boundary of a compartment or threatens values within.	Point or perimeter protection	Use aircraft to drop retardant and or water to stop or slow the spread of fire towards the critical point. Use engines and tractors as needed. Pumps and irrigations systems may be set up to aid in protection when time and terrain permit.

- **Hazardous Fuels**

Hazardous fuel reduction projects may include prescribed burning, mechanical and herbicide treatments. Specific fuel treatment objectives for Swanquarter FMU include:

1. Conduct prescribed burns in all established burn units striving for a 3-5 year fire return interval.

2. Work with the NCWRC to reduce hazardous fuels and restore the disturbance role of fire in fire-adapted plant communities in Unit 2.5.1 in conjunction with Gull Rock Gamelands, striving to establish a 3-7 year fire return interval.

3. Consider wilderness values and Minimum Impact Suppression Tactics (MIST) when developing Prescribed Fire Plans for wilderness areas.

4. Maintain the Bell Island and North Boundary Roads as needed in preparation for wildfire control, prescribed burn treatments, road maintenance, and access needs.

- **Desired Future Vegetation Conditions**

  1. Maintain the pine woodlands in the North and Central Bell Island Burn Units (2.2.1-2.2.2) as open pine savannahs.

  2. Maintain or restore marsh to have a diversity of plant species beneficial to waterfowl and shorebirds.

  3. Maintain, or restore where necessary, the Wilderness Area to pre-settlement conditions, including fire frequency, while acknowledging that the effects of sea level rise must also be considered.

3.3.4. Swanquarter FMU Safety Considerations

Marshes are characterized by flashy grass and shrub fuels which can sustain extremely rapid rates of spread with intense heat generated. Swamps and pocosins at Swanquarter NWR contain heavy shrub and timber fuels, some of which are often prone to extreme fire behavior, particularly where never before burned. Access and vehicle trafficability in this FMU is very poor in most places. More of the FMU is accessible by boat than by vehicle due to limited roads and trafficability for equipment. Escape routes and safety zones are scarce with large water sources providing the best safety zones. Because of the potential for re-burn in shrub and timber fuels, only well burned, blackened areas should be considered safe.

Most of the FMU is open to the public, but is only accessible by boat, canoe, or kayak. The graveled Bell Island Road provides public access to the Bell Island pier. Fishing from the pier and adjacent waters is open year-round.

US 264 is a major transportation corridor in the county and is a paved, two-lane road with narrow shoulders that lies to the north of the refuge. The road is very curvy and is often used by wide farm tractors that can make passing difficult and dangerous. The road does not receive heavy traffic, but vehicle traffic is constant enough to be a concern for smoke impacts and firefighter safety.

3.4. Fire Management Unit 3 – Cedar Island NWR

Table 7: 10-Year Average by Fiscal Year (1999-2008) for Wildland Fire Management Activities on Cedar Island NWR

Type	Number	Acres
Wildfires	2.5	456.6
Prescribed Burns	3.1	2036.6
Non-Fire Projects	3.1	29.0

3.4.1. Cedar Island FMU Characteristics

Cedar Island NWR (14,395 burnable acres) is located along Pamlico Sound in Carteret County. The refuge supports approximately 11,000 acres of saltmarsh, 3,395 acres of forest, and 85 acres of cleared land. Most forest is shrub pocosin with uplands supporting scattered stands of longleaf pine and wiregrass. Fuels are classified as tall grass (FM 3), pocosin shrub (FM 4,6) and timber (FM 7,9). Locally developed fuel model maps are shown in Figure 7. Soils at Cedar Island NWR are shallow and underlain with peat.

The refuge has Memoranda of Understanding with two private landowners and the Cherry Point Marine Corps Air Station (MCAS) to conduct prescribed burns in Burn Units that include both refuge land and other ownership. The refuge is adjacent to the Outlying Atlantic Field and close to Piney Island, both of which are operated by the Cherry Point Marine Corps Air Station. These military areas have been the source of several wildfires caused by flares and have sensitive equipment that could be threatened by a wildfire leaving the refuge.

Table 8: Burn Unit Acres by Ownership in Cedar Island FMU

Ownership	Acres
Cedar Island NWR	14,495
Non-refuge	1,009
Total in FMU	15,489

The refuge is divided into Fire Compartments and Burn Units which are delineated on Figure 12 (see Section 4.2). Sixty-three wildfires have occurred on Cedar Island NWR since 1968. These fires ranged in size from 0.1 acres to 6,000 acres. Known causes include: lightning, military flares, and arson. Since 1994, the total acres managed with prescribed fire have grown steadily from a few hundred acres to include most of the contiguous landbase on the refuge. By 2007, the majority of refuge lands had been burned with exception of the North Fire Compartment, Units 3.1.1 and 3.1.8 in the Northwest Fire Compartment, and a 30 acre tract behind the Cedar Island Fire Department in the Lola Fire Compartment. Since then, the majority of the refuge has been burned on roughly a 5-year return interval, with burning efforts hampered by drought conditions allowing fewer burn windows and budget concerns that limit the availability of resources.

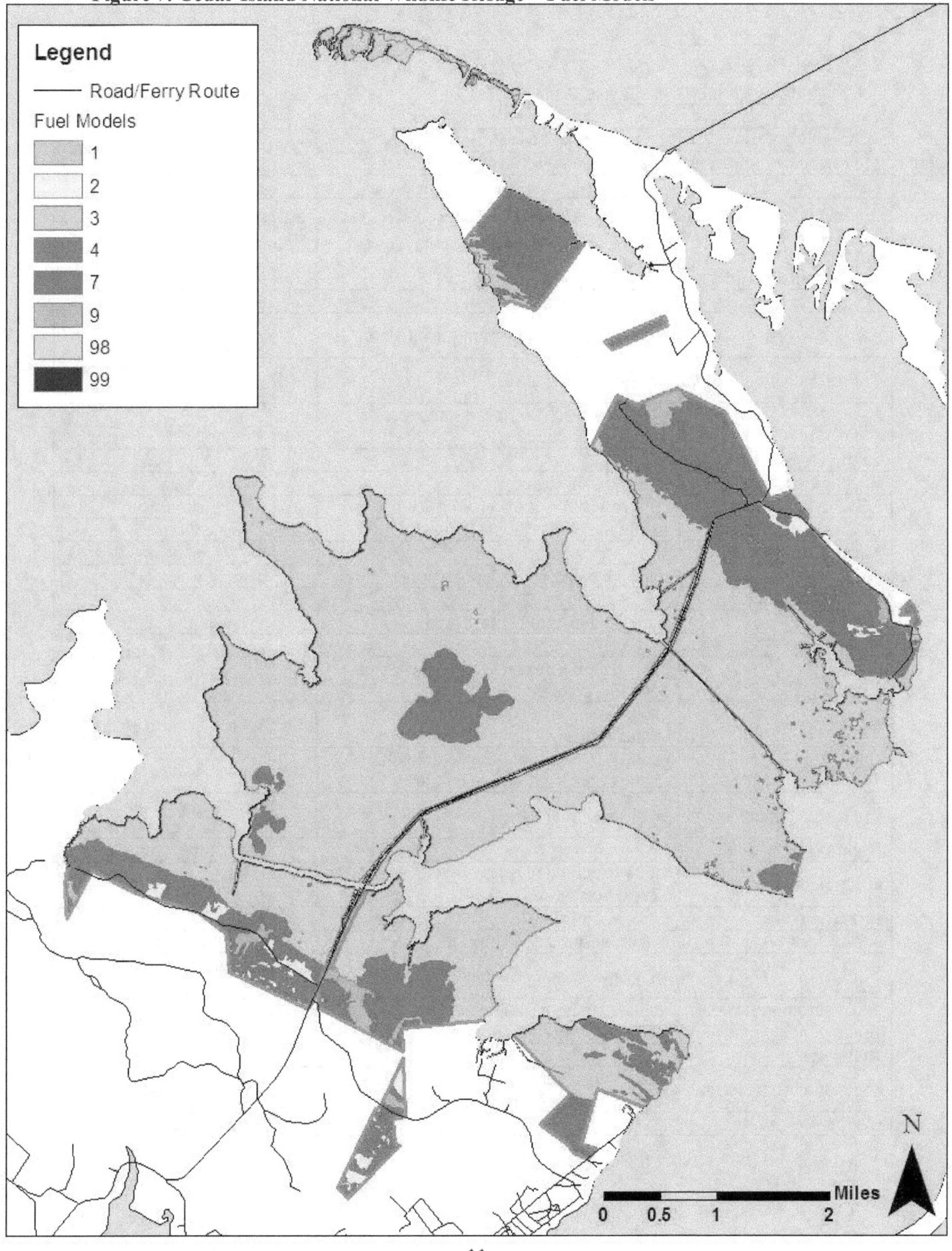

3.4.2. Cedar Island FMU Values to Protect

Values to Protect	Description	Risk
Threatened & Endangered Species		
RCW	potential habitat in long leaf pine areas	endangered species
Air Quality		
Carteret County communities and transportation corridors	potential smoke impacts to air quality and visibility	life, human health, socio-economic impacts
WUI		
Atlantic	state recognized Community At Risk (CAR)	life, property, human health, socio-economic impacts
Cedar Island	state recognized CAR	life, property, human health, socio-economic impacts
building	wood fish shack NC 12 at south side of Thorofare bridge	property
Cultural Resources		
shell midens	5 shell miden sites	cultural
Lola Radar Station	20th century Naval tower	historical
Downing cemetery	small family cemetery at ?	cultural
Natural Resources		
Wetlands	sensitive organic soils and estuarine values	natural, water quality
Special Designations		
SNHA	significant natural heritage area	natural, wildlife
Recreation		
waterfowl hunting	public hunting available in 400 acre area north of Thorofare Canal	life, human health, recreation
fishing	public fishing available in sound waters around refuge	life, human health, recreation
boat ramps	public boat ramps at Lola Road (with floating dock) and Thorofare Canal	life, human health, recreation
kiosk and entrance signs	NC 12 and Lola Rd.	recreation, government property
Right-of-ways		
utility right-of-way	utility poles and telephone boxes along NC 12 and Lola Road	utilities
Infrastructure		
NC 12	major transportation corridor	highway safety
Ferry Dock at Cedar Island	ferry landing and offices	government property, human health
communications tower at Atlantic Field	military communications tower and electronics site	government property
Refuge property		
office and visitor center	refuge office, maintenance compound, storage buildings, visitor brochures	government property
weather station	RAWS	government property

3.4.3. Cedar Island FMU Management Guidance

- **AMR**

Cedar Island NWR currently has one non-fire qualified maintenance worker assigned to the refuge. Excluding the VFDs, the closest firefighting resources are the NCDFR stationed approximately one-hour from the refuge. The next closest resources are stationed at Croatan National Forest and Cherry Point MCAS, approximately 1.5 hours away. The closest FWS resources are at Mattamuskeet and Pocosin Lakes NWR, about 3 hours away. This distance from resources has led to designating the NCDFR in our AOP with primary suppression responsibilities on the refuge. When NCDFR responds to a wildfire on the refuge it will simultaneously contact FWS resources.

The table below gives examples of potential AMRs for the Cedar Island FMU. Specific AMR objectives for this FMU include:

1. Protect communities and private structures through cooperation with the NCDFR, local VFDs, and Cherry Point MCAS.

2. Work with NCDFR, VFDs, and other cooperators to ensure their cooperation and by-in to refuge approved AMR.

FMU 3 Appropriate Management Response

Potential situations	Potential strategies	Potential tactics
Fire burning in accessible area near a road or water access, small enough to conduct direct attack.	Direct attack	Use engines to suppress fires near roads, portable pumps and boats to suppress fires with water access. Tractor/plows may be used on upland sites and in pocosins. Marshmasters and tractors without plows may be used in marsh if deemed safe and expedient to suppress the fire.
Fire occurs or escapes into one of the interior sections of compartments.	Indirect attack.	Use engines and tractors to hold or burn out critical control lines as needed. Monitor or burn out remainder of fuels in compartment as needed.
Fire occurs or escapes into one of the interior sections of compartments.	Monitor the fire, establishing Management Action Points with trigger points and pre-determined response plans.	Monitor with aircraft. Use aerially applied retardant, or water, engines and tractors as holding resources as needed to keep the fire contained within the compartment.
Fire threatens to escape the boundary of a compartment or threatens values within.	Point protection	Use aircraft to drop retardant and or water to stop or slow the spread of fire towards the critical point. Use engines and tractors as needed. Use water and foam or chippers to pre-treat fuels around values at risk if time available.

- **Hazardous Fuels**

Hazardous fuel reduction projects may include prescribed burning, mechanical and herbicide treatments. Specific fuel treatment objectives for Cedar Island FMU include:

1. Conduct prescribed burns in designated burn units, striving for a 3-5 year fire return interval to reduce hazardous fuels in the wildland-urban interface and meet habitat management objectives.

2. Enhance long leaf pine savannah habitat by burning these acres on a 1 to 3 year fire return interval for potential future use by threatened and endangered species (e.g. red-cockaded woodpecker and other key management species) and migratory birds.

3. Initiate growing season burns when and where appropriate to mimic natural fire seasonality and maximize fire effects.

4. Annually maintain 76 acres of roads and firebreaks as needed in this FMU in preparation for wildfire control, prescribed burn treatments, and road maintenance.

- **Desired Future Vegetation Conditions**

1. Frequent burning in Longleaf Pine stands should once again expand this historical vegetation type out across areas now dominated by other pine species and shrubs, particularly in the margins of the sandy uplands where pocosin shrub, pond pine and loblolly pine have encroached with fire exclusion over the past 50 years. Wiregrass communities should become re-established in conjunction with longleaf restoration.

2. Marshes should show a greater diversity of grassland vegetation, particularly on the upper elevation marsh sites.

3. Pocosins should show a greater diversity of shrub structure and age class, with early successional bogs and grasslands interspersed within.

3.4.4. Cedar Island FMU Safety Considerations

The fuels at Cedar Island NWR are capable of high rates of spread, particularly when they are exposed to the frequently strong winds. Those areas with a 3-5 year rough can sustain extreme rates of spread and high intensity burning while areas within a couple of years of prescribed burning normally show reduced fire intensity due to the modified fuels. During seasonally dry periods, organic soils may sustain combustion and hold fire even after a rain event until conditions dry out again and can sustain spread. There are numerous snags in the timber stands and pocosins which pose hazards to firefighters and increased risk of escape for fires.

Access and trafficability in this FMU is very poor. The thick tangled shrub pocosins and wooded areas outside where recent burns have taken place may present special challenges. The firebreaks and dirt roads which access the burn units can be very wet and hard to travel. The marshes are most easily accessed by boat or marshmaster. Escape routes and safety zones are scarce with large water sources providing the best safety zones. Because of the potential for re-burn in these fuels, only well burned, blackened areas should be considered safe.

Most of the FMU is open to the public, but is only accessible by foot or by boat, canoe, or kayak. NC Highway 12 bisects the refuge and terminates in the Community of Cedar Island at the NC DOT Ferry Dock. NC 12 is a paved, two-lane highway with narrow shoulders. This popular ferry and road serve as a gateway to the Core Banks area and Moorehead City. It is a major concern for traffic hazards caused by smoke and safety to firefighters conducting fire management activities alongside the road. NC 12 and Lola Road serve as access through the refuge and points from which to observe wildlife. On the south side of the refuge, Old Cedar Island Road takes local traffic from NC-12 east to the community of Atlantic and through a portion of the refuge. The refuge is open to waterfowl hunting with many private blinds surrounding the refuge out in the Sound. There is a public boat ramp maintained by the refuge at the end of Lola Road and one at the Thorofare Canal.

4.0 Wildland Fire Operational Guidance

Fire management operations planned and conducted pursuant to this FMP will follow the policies and guidelines of the *Redbook* and *FWS Fire Management Handbook*.

The Mattamuskeet Complex has one fire-funded employee based at Mattamuskeet NWR. This employee works together with operations and maintenance, resource, and management personnel to support the Mattamuskeet Complex's fire program. They work closely with the other refuges and cooperators within the FWS Southeast Region Fire Management District 1 to conduct fire suppression operations and fuel treatment projects on national wildlife refuges and on cooperator's lands within the constraints of cooperative agreements. Complex fire qualified personnel and the positions for which they qualify are listed in the Annual Operations Plan. Fire-funded personnel that are responsible for district-wide duties are based at Alligator River, Pocosin Lakes, Mattamuskeet and Mackay Island NWRs. The duties of all fire staff in District 1, whether District or Refuge employees, include the following:
- work together and with other refuge staff and cooperators to provide the primary staffing necessary for making an appropriate management response on wildfires,
- perform planning and preparedness duties,
- maintain fire facilities and equipment, and
- plan, prepare for and implement prescribed burns on refuge and cooperator lands..

District 1 Personnel:
- District Fire Management Officer (DFMO) – responsible for the overall coordination and oversight for the Fire Management Program in Fire District 1. The DFMO supervises the District fire personnel and the Alligator River NWR fire crew.
- Fire Program Administrative Assistant – responsible for assisting the DFMO in accounting and fire budgeting, and serves as the primary Dispatcher for District 1. Assists with payroll, AD hires, purchases and personnel actions.
- Prescribed Fire Specialist (PFS) – responsible for overall coordination of the prescribed fire program in District 1 and specifically responsible for fire management program coordination on the Mattamuskeet Complex.

- Wildland Urban Interface Specialist (WUIS) – responsible for administering fire assistance programs with rural fire departments and coordinating wildland fire issues with communities near Refuges. The WUIS serves as the Fire Planner for the District.

Alligator River NWR Staff:
- Supervisory Forestry Technician (Fire Control Officer) - supervises fire operations at ARNWR/PINWR and serves as an equipment management coordinator and trainer for District 1.
- Three Engineering Equipment Operators – Fire
- Two Forestry Technicians – Fire

Pocosin Lakes NWR Staff:
- Refuge Fire Management Officer - supervises fire operations at Pocosin Lakes NWR and serves as Assistant District FMO when needed. Serves as District 1 Training Officer and subject matter expert on smoke management and fire environment issues.
- Three Engineering Equipment Operators – Fire
- Two Forestry Technicians – Fire

Mattamuskeet NWR Staff:
- One Forestry Technician – Fire

Mackay Island NWR Staff:
- One Forestry Technician - Fire

The *Redbook* and *FWS Fire Management Handbook* spell out the fire management responsibilities for the Regional Director, Regional Fire Management Coordinator, Project Leader, and Refuge Fire Management Officer. Policy also allows for certain authorities to be delegated from the Agency Administrator to the District Fire Management Officer (Appendix G). The remaining fire-funded members of the Fire Management Team have duties established through their position descriptions and annual performance plans. Fire qualification goals and trainings are worked out with individual fire-funded and collateral team members when employees' Individual Development Plans are developed for the year. A current copy of the approved District 1 Fire Staffing Chart and a description of Fire Team responsibilities are included in Appendix H.

Goals for the development of the Refuge Fire Management Team are:

1. Develop Safety as the number one awareness issue within the fire program on the Complex.

2. Develop/maintain appropriate level of staffing of trained and qualified firefighting personnel to meet the fire management needs of the three refuges, within funding constraints.

3. Develop and organize available resources on the refuges and within the District into an experienced fire organization capable of safely attacking wildfires with a successful control rate of 95%. Refuge resources must be able to interface with cooperators and outside FWS resources to successfully control the remaining 5%. Selected refuge staff will be trained and developed to assist other refuges and interagency cooperators locally, regionally, and nationally.

4. Actively seek ways to encourage and develop cooperative relationships with NCDFR, U.S. Forest Service (USFS), local Volunteer Fire Departments, DOD, Emergency Management, and local law enforcement agencies. Cooperative relations must be mutually beneficial to all parties in an agreement, result in more effective protection of values from threat or loss from wildfire, and improve safety for all wildland firefighters.

4.1. Appropriate Management Response (AMR)

Safety is the number one priority in all fire suppression actions. The 10 Standard Fire Orders and 18 Watch Out Situations will be the guide in all fire operations. Structural fire suppression is the responsibility of local governments. We may assist with exterior structural protection activities under formal Fire Protection Agreements that specify mutual responsibilities, including funding (*Redbook* 01-3).

A Wildland Fire Situation Analysis (WFSA) or other appropriate analysis tool will be prepared for any wildfire that escapes initial attack. Multi-jurisdictional incidents will require a collaboratively developed WFSA that is approved and signed by each of the respective agencies.

The wildfires on the Mattamuskeet Complex have varied greatly in size with small wildfires managed as Type 4 incidents punctuated by larger incidents of varying complexity under a Type 3 organization. An NWCG complexity analysis will be completed on all incidents to determine the appropriate level of management organization. Higher complexity incidents may result in Type 2 incident management teams being ordered. Complexity factors for incidents that rank out as higher complexity would likely be influenced by impacts to human communities and multiple jurisdictional involvement and the expected duration of the fire. The extent and severity of ground fire is often the deciding factor in the duration and complexity of an incident. Ground fire of any size may have detrimental effects to the neighboring communities due to health concerns (smoke) and difficulty of containment. It may last for months before it is extinguished by suppression efforts or precipitation, and any ground fire suppression will be very expensive due to the duration of the tractor and water moving operations. Suppression costs will always be subordinate to values to protect for fires that escape refuge boundaries and threaten residences, businesses and private timber resources. Increasing WUI areas on or adjacent to all refuges could easily see the complexity of wildfire events increase in the future. Details on refuge fire history can be found in the refuge files or in FMIS.

4.1.1. AMR Direction

- **General AMR Direction**

All wildfires will receive an AMR as quickly as possible. AMR is the response to a wildland fire that most effectively, efficiently, and safely meets objectives identified in this approved Fire Management Plan. Evaluation and selection of an AMR to a wildfire will include consideration of risks to public and firefighter safety, threats to the values to protect, the cost of the various mitigation strategies and tactics, and the potential resource benefits. Refer to Sections 3.2 – 3.4 under each FMU for specific direction.

The response may range across a spectrum of strategic options including the following examples:

- A monitoring strategy would entail periodic reconnoitering of the fire to ensure that it does not threaten key values or escape into another compartment or area.

- Indirect attack strategies use existing or constructed fire breaks to burn out and hold key areas of terrain so that the fire cannot escape from a particular compartment or area.

- Direct attack strategies use ground and/or aviation resources directly engaged in the immediate fire environment in order to contain or slow the fire to prevent it from escaping an area or affecting key values to protect.

- A point protection strategy is often used to protect high values when a fast moving fire threatens and time is critical.

At times, more than one or perhaps all these strategic responses may be required in combination to meet the needs for an AMR. Often burning out sections of an area or an entire compartment will be the most effective strategy to ensure containment. Tactical operations to accomplish an AMR may include the use of aircraft, low ground pressure fire tractors, tracked brush cutters, engines, boats, and fire crews using hand tools, ignition devices or portable pumps. Due to accessibility and the volatile nature of pocosin and marsh fuels, only tactics that can ensure the safety of all assigned personnel and that pose a good probability for success will be selected for an AMR.

Smoke impacts to Smoke Sensitive Areas (see Section 4.2.1.5.) will be a consideration when choosing an AMR. Potential smoke impacts can include visibility hazards and/or public health impacts. When smoke impacts are expected, fire mangers will attempt to work with interagency partners to monitor smoke and inform the public of any associated hazards.

Because of heavy fuels and organic soils in pocosins, once a fire is contained it still has a high probability for escape. Specific steps must be taken to ensure the success of holding resources. Often the first step is to widen firelines with multiple tractors plowing lines around the perimeter. Sometimes vegetation is masticated with chippers or sheared and piled with dozers with KG blades to widen the control lines. Next, if conditions are fairly dry in the upper soil and duff layer, sprinkler systems will be installed using irrigation equipment and pumps deployed from nearby canals. If an area can be flooded using landscape-scale water management techniques, this will be the next option. Hose lays with engines and portable pumps are used if the area is not extremely dry or has predominantly mineral soils. These methods may be used separately or together on any fire to attempt to achieve successful holding operations. Regardless of the type of AMR, leaders must ensure that decisions are timely and actions are decisive. All actively burning wildfires will monitored, and then staffed as needed until declared controlled or out.

All wildfires will be supervised by a qualified Incident Commander (IC) responsible to

- Assess the fire situation and make a report to dispatch as soon as possible.
- Use guidance in this FMP or a Delegation of Authority to determine and implement an appropriate management response.
- Determine organization, resource needs, strategy and tactics.
- Brief incoming and assigned resources on the organization, strategy and tactics, weather and fire behavior, LCES, and radio frequencies.

- Order resources needed for the AMR through the designated dispatch office.
- Manage the incident until relieved or the incident is under control.

The FMP and a delegation of authority with an associated WFSA from the agency administrator can provide a general strategy to an IC, who has discretion to select and implement appropriate tactics within the limits described for the FMU(s), including when and where to use minimum impact suppression tactics (MIST) unless otherwise specified. Each wildland fire is unique with its own set of weather, fire behavior, resource, and event variables that must be taken into consideration by the IC when choosing an AMR. Impacts to the land and cost considerations will always be considered in fire management planning, but will take second priority to firefighter and public safety. All resources, including mutual aid resources, will report to the IC (in person or by radio) and receive a briefing and assignment prior to tactical deployment.

- **General AMR Constraints**

1. Aerial or ground application of fire retardants, foams, and water enhancers should be avoided within 300 feet of waterways unless life or property is threatened and their use can reasonably be expected to alleviate the threat. Other exceptions can be found in Chapter 12 of the *Redbook*.

2. Use of retardant, foam, and aircraft in wilderness, RNA, and other special areas will require approval from the Refuge Manager.

3. The Refuge Manager is the decision authority for equipment use in wilderness areas on Swanquarter NWR and Research Natural Areas (RNA) on Mattamuskeet NWR. Use of heavy equipment in wilderness areas will require Regional Office concurrence.

4. Agency firefighters will not take direct suppression actions on structure, vehicle, or landfill fires, but limit firefighting efforts to areas where the fire has spread onto agency protected lands.

5. Refuge equipment will be washed prior to leaving the District and before returning to help prevent the spread of invasive species.

6. Extreme fire weather conditions occur more frequently in the coastal areas of the State due to especially strong winds. Also, large water bodies in close proximity to the refuges create localized winds that can defy general and spot weather forecasts.

7. Organic soils which are prone to ignite and cause significant impacts.

8. The remoteness of Cedar Island NWR, which takes 3-5 driving hours for FWS fire resources to reach, always increases response time and costs for wildland fire activities.

9. Wetland soils and protection considerations must be taken into account on all fire management activities.

10. Access and availability of specialized equipment capable of working in the wetland soils is always a factor in wildland fire activities.

- **Interagency Operations**

The statewide interagency *Master Agreement* and the AOP for interagency resources in the District spell out how non-refuge resources will respond to wildland fires on Mattamuskeet, Swanquarter, and Cedar Island NWRs. Following the closest resource concept, the NCDFR will make an initial response to wildfires at Cedar Island NWR while simultaneously informing the Service. The Forestry Division employed by USMC at Cherry Point Marine Corps Air Station (MCAS) is a primary cooperator, especially at Cedar Island NWR. A Memorandum of Understanding (MOU) for fire management between the MCAS and Cedar Island NWR covers both wildfire suppression and prescribed burning. Through annual cooperative meetings, refuge staff will make cooperators and partners aware of the AMR for these refuges.

Pre-attack planning will focus on continuing the excellent cooperation between the FWS and the NCDFR, as well as continuing to develop cooperative relations with the Volunteer Fire Departments and local Emergency Management. Some of this planning will be captured in the AOP or in Community Wildfire Protection Plans (CWPP) as they are developed. Local and agency law enforcement personnel will be utilized as needed to protect the public and to close portions of a refuge to the public during wildfire incidents if necessary.

Refuge	Cooperating Fire Department
Swanquarter NWR	Swan Quarter VFD
Cedar Island NWR	Cedar Island VFD
Cedar Island NWR	Atlantic VFD

4.1.2. Preparedness

- **Fire Management Planning**

District fire staff in conjunction with refuge managers will annually update the FMP and appendices as needed and review pre-incident planning to resolve as many logistical and operational questions as possible in advance of a major incident. District staff will update the District Station Aviation Plan every two years or as needed to update the Aerial Hazards Maps and incorporate policy changes. All interagency agreements will be reviewed to ensure currency and relevancy to the fire management needs of the refuges and our partners.

- **National Fire Danger Rating System (NFDRS)**

The NFDRS is a set of numeric indices that describe the potential over a given geographic area for fires to ignite, spread, and require fire suppression action. Fire weather information is integrated with fuel and topographic information to calculate NFDRS indices. To establish the initial indices for the District, weather data for the years 1998-2008 from the Alligator River NWR (ALR) and Pocosin Lakes NWR (POR) RAWS (Remote Access Weather Station) were processed with the FireFamily Plus program (See Figure 8). This program identifies staffing level breakpoints for use in the District's Step-up Plan.

Figure 8: Graphs of the Mean NFDRS values (BI, ERC, and KBDI) and fuel moistures calculated using Fire Family Plus software. Weather data uses an average of the Alligator River NWR (ALR) and Pocosin Lakes NWR (POR) RAWS data with equal weighting (1998-2008).

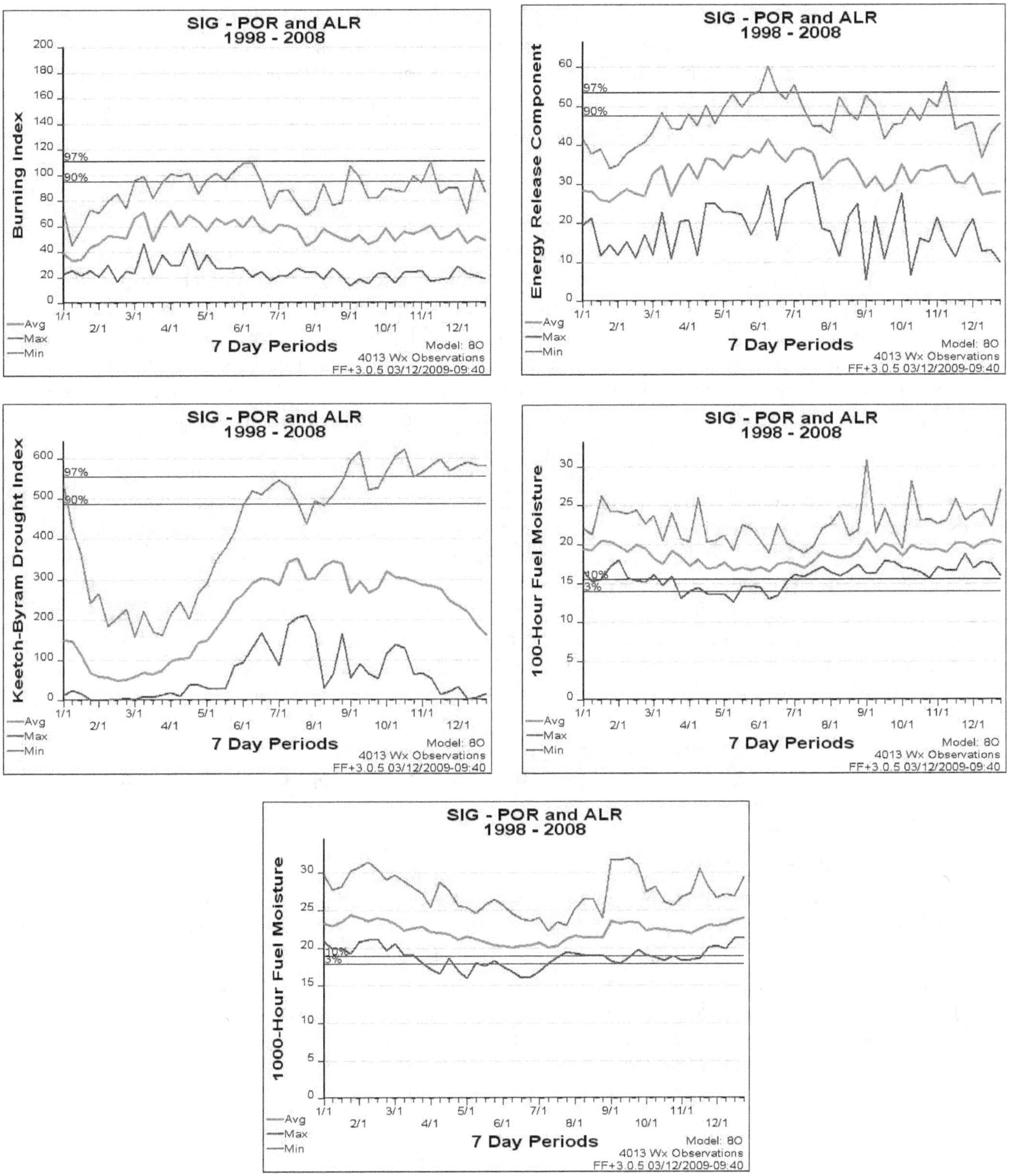

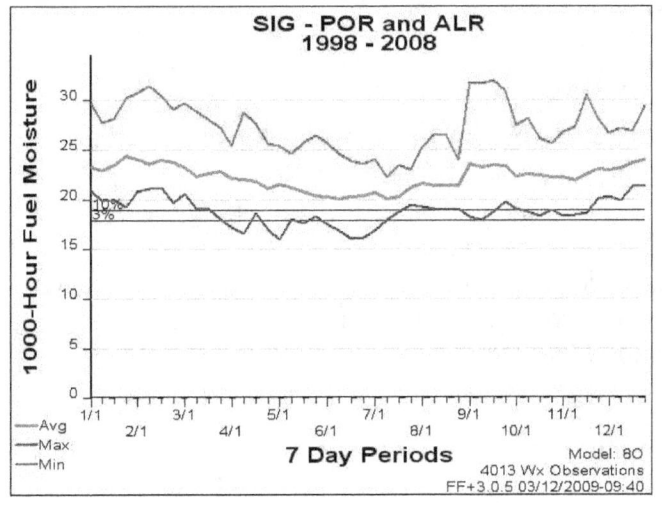

Of the indices available through the NFDRS, Burning Index (BI) has been selected as the basis to rank fire danger in the Service's Southeast Region. Burning Index therefore provides the basis for increased readiness and determining staffing class levels. BI, defined as flame length times 10, is designed to reflect the difficulty in controlling a new fire start. It is driven by the variables of wind speed and fine dead fuel moisture, which in turn are directly related to relative humidity. BI (and all NFDRS outputs) relate only to the potential of an initiating fire that spreads, without crowning or spotting, through continuous fuels on a uniform slope. Additional NFDRS indices, such as Energy Release Component (ERC) and Keetch-Byrum Drought Index (KBDI) will be used in determining Step-up Plan staffing levels.

- **Step-up Plan**

Step-up Plans are designed to direct incremental preparedness actions in response to increasing fire danger. "Staffing Levels" delineate those actions. The level of fire danger is expressed as a "Preparedness Level", which is determined by incremental measures of burning conditions, fire activity, and resource commitment. The refuges' predetermined responses to increased fire danger for a burning period follows District 1's Step-up Plan found in Appendix A. Staffing levels correlate directly to preparedness levels and the terms are used interchangeably. Given the small number of fire-qualified Complex staff and where they are located, successful initial attack will not occur without the assistance of firefighters from other refuges in the District.

Fire managers will participate with interagency partners in sharing and coordinating weather station information relating to fire danger assessments. A RAWS at Cedar Island NWR will be used in conjunction with other area weather stations to assess fire danger on the Mattamuskeet Complex. The District Dispatch Office will keep Refuge and District personnel appraised of fire danger and weather conditions, ensuring all stations are aware of current fire danger and are taking appropriate actions. This function will be monitored by the District FMO to ensure responsiveness and consistency in the program. Members of the Mattamuskeet Complex fire staff will assist other refuges as members of the Fire Management District 1 Fire Team as needed for wildfire assignments.

If National and Regional preparedness levels reach 4 or 5, the District may step-up a level in preparedness as a result. This will also signal that prescribed burning activities may need to be postponed or receive Regional concurrence.

- **Emergency Preparedness**

During the fire season there will be short-term weather events and increased human activity that increase fire danger beyond what may be predicted for the Step-up Plan. These types of events cannot be planned or budgeted and may call for lengthening the duty day, extending the work week, or detailing extra resources to meet the anticipated danger. The District FMO has the authority to make this decision with notification to the Regional Fire Management Coordinator. Limitations on utilizing emergency preparedness funds are listed in the *Redbook* Chapter 10 and the *FWS Fire Management Handbook*.

- **Severity**

Severity funds are available subject to the National Fire Coordinator's approval whenever there is a longer term high fire danger event, such as a drought that extends or prolongs the normal fire season or causes a severe strain on normal refuge activities due to higher staffing requirements, or an above average wildfire activity that has a "drawdown" effect on local suppression forces. Severity requests will be done on a District basis. Severity funds may be requested whenever the KBDI exceeds the 532 level and or staffing needs exceed those that can be supported by the District. If ongoing wildfires are tying up resources (FWS and cooperators) for extended periods of time, and the local refuges are having difficulty meeting minimum staffing needs, they may request severity funds at lower KBDI levels.

All incoming resources arriving on severity details (as with all other incidents) will be briefed prior to being assigned. This briefing will cover this FMP as well as local fire cards, expected fire behavior, tactics, communications and other necessary information.

- **Training and Qualifications**

Refuge staff on the Mattamuskeet Complex are all encouraged to pursue and fill fire qualifications for which they are able. They must meet the medical standards for firefighters, including a physical, before they can be declared fit for duty. Agency firefighting personnel are encouraged to participate in a fitness program for which they are allowed official duty time for physical training depending on their fitness qualification. Firefighters are required to pass a Work Capacity Test appropriate for their qualification skill.

Annual training is geared to increase the safety awareness, technical skill, and fire-job qualifications of firefighters in the Fire District. All training is oriented to the NWCG standards. Requirements for annual refreshers and physical and medical testing are provided in *National Interagency Incident Management System Wildfire Qualification System Guide* (also known as 310-1, http://www.nwcg.gov/pms/docs/pms-310-1_2008.pdf) or listed in the *FWS Fire Management Handbook*. Each employee has an IDP which is developed annually with their supervisor to determine training and development needs including fire related training needed for skill and leader positions. Training is obtained through cooperators and Regional and National interagency training courses. Often, one or two 200-level courses are taught yearly by district firefighters. The NCDFR offers 200 and 300-level training courses across the state, most of which meet NWCG requirements. Additional training needs are obtained by sending personnel to interagency training coordinated through the State and Regional Coordination Centers or cooperators. As a minimum, the Annual Firefighter Safety Refresher training is offered prior to the Spring Fire Season.

- **Readiness**

Prior to the beginning of the established fire season, a readiness evaluation must be conducted to evaluate detection, communication, dispatch and response capabilities. The DFMO will use the *Fire and Aviation Preparedness Review Guide* provided by BLM as a format to determine and document pre-season readiness. This document can be found at http://www.blm.gov/nifc/st/en/prog/fire/fireops/preparedness/preparedness_review.html.

The only fire dedicated facilities on the Mattamuskeet Complex are a military storage container at Mattamuskeet NWR used as a fire cache and a 2-bay metal storage building at Cedar Island NWR. However, a new shop is under construction at Mattamuskeet NWR which will be completed in 2010. This shop will have one bay devoted to the fire program for storage of an engine and fire cache. Fire cache and equipment will be maintained in readiness condition year-round on the refuges because of the nature of fire occurrences and prescribed burning activities. A fire cache inventory at Mattamuskeet NWR will be kept up-to-date reflecting the items in the cache at all times with an annually updated list kept in the Dispatch Office. Normally the cache will be replenished after each wildfire and prescribed burn season in coordination with the DFMO. Orders reflecting emergency needs will be made any time. As funds and staff allow, a second cache with additional equipment will be set up at Cedar Island NWR.

The Dispatch office at Alligator River NWR serves as the District Dispatch Office for the entire Fire Management District. The District Dispatch Office will be staffed on all PL-III (Preparedness Level III) days or higher during the fire season and on demand during the remainder of the year. A description of Dispatch duties is included in the Appendix and the AOP includes a discussion on how the Office will interact with our interagency partners.

Table 9: Annual Refuge Fire Preparedness Activities

Activities – Complete before end of month	J	F	M	A	M	J	J	A	S	O	N	D
Fire Equipment Inspections	X	X	X	X	X	X	X	X	X	X	X	X
Update Interagency Fire Agreements/AOPs	X											
Inventory Fire Engine and Cache		X										
Annual Refresher Training			X									
Pre-Season Engine Preparation and Inventory			X							X		
Weigh Engines to verify GVW Compliance			X									
Equipment Preparation and Maintenance			X									
Annual Medical Examinations										X	X	
Annual Fitness Testing			X									
Annual Work Plan for upcoming FY						X						
Prescribed Fire Plans Preparation					X	X	X	X	X			
Weather Station Maintenance and Calibration										X		
PLDO Annual Refresher										X		
Complete Training Analysis										X		
Review and Update FMP and Appendices												X
Winterize Fire Management Equipment												X
Aircraft Pre-Accident Plan	X						X					

- **Community Assistance**

The DFMO will work with the District Wildland-Urban Interface Specialist (WUIS) to identify community assistance projects and grant programs (e.g., Rural Fire Assistance, Ready Reserve, or Firewise) for funding consideration. The District WUIS will also work with refuge staff, communities and cooperators to establish Community Wildfire Protection Plans (CWPP) and/or Firewise Communities/USA Mitigation Plans that detail project actions and responsibilities for community protection. Cooperators will be consulted for project prioritization and coordination of efforts. The District WUIS will work with refuge staff to ensure implementation of any funded projects.

- **Fire Season**

Wildfires can occur on the Mattamuskeet Complex at any time of year as evidenced by fire history. The primary season of consistently high fire danger is March 1 through August 1 when high winds, low humidity and low fuel moisture create optimal conditions for wildfires. Ignition sources during this time of year are normally agricultural burning on adjoining property, lightning, arson, and military use. During drought years, high fire occurrence in Eastern North Carolina can extend into the fall and even winter months. During this extended season, military and agricultural operations are the primary ignition sources.

Figure 9: The total number of wildfires by month on Mattamuskeet (MTR), Swanquarter (SWR), and Cedar Island (CDR) NWRs. Fire data is from FMIS from 1980-2008.

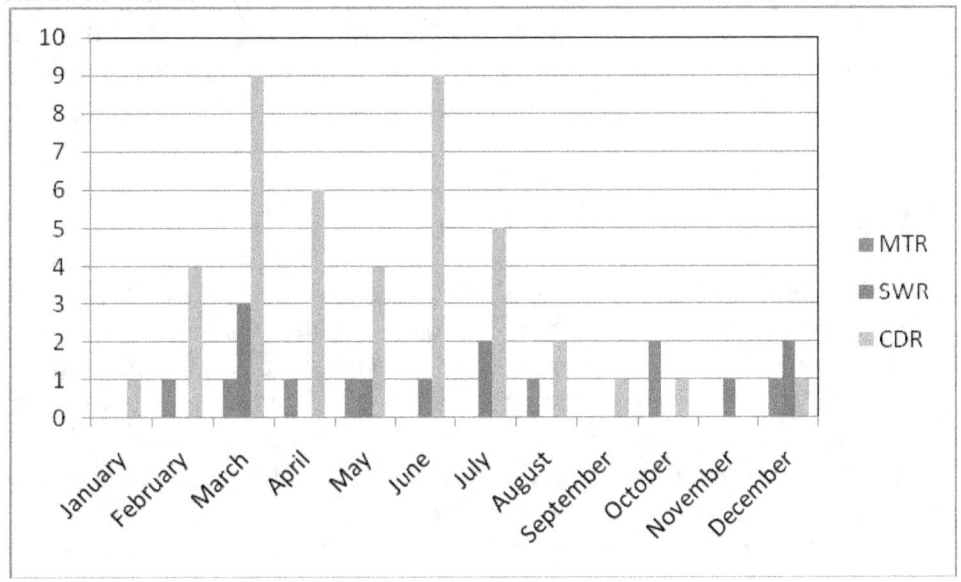

4.1.3. Detection

Refuge resources are not normally used exclusively for detection purposes. Fires are primarily discovered through aerial detection flights or called into 911 by local citizens.

No fire team in Eastern North Carolina would be complete without a competent air-attack qualified pilot in a light, maneuverable aircraft. The pilot must be skilled in fire suppression tactics, fire behavior in local fuels, and directing ground resources by two-way radio communication. The pilot needs to be knowledgeable of equipment capabilities in heavy fuels with marginal trafficability in wetland soils.

The NPS pilot and aircraft stationed at the Cape Hatteras National Seashore (NS) have in the past met this criteria. As long as the NS maintains a pilot position with fire qualifications, this pilot and aircraft will be used for performing aerial detection flights in the District. Detection flights are done once or twice daily on PL-III or higher days during the regular fire season and on an intermittent basis during the remainder of the year. Once a smoke is spotted, the pilot contacts the District Dispatch Office to report the location and give a size-up of the fire. Often the pilot will direct personnel into the fire, watching for their safety serving the function of a lookout. If additional air resources are needed, a qualified air attack pilot will be requested.

Refuge detection flights will be coordinated with detection flights flown by the NCDFR to avoid duplication. NCDFR pilots are trained to report any fires or smokes that they discover on Service lands when flying their regular patrol flights. When NPS aircraft is unavailable, vendor aircraft that meet the DOI National Business Center – Aviation Management Directorate requirements may be ordered though contract arrangements to assist with aerial detection and wildfire response. A qualified aviation manager will be used as required and needed to direct the flights.

4.1.4. Dispatch, Initial Response and Initial Attack

All wildland fires will be reported to the Dispatch Office at Alligator River NWR. Usually human-caused wildfires will be located either on a road shoulder, dike or sound shore, but lightning fires can show up anywhere and are often a good distance off the highway. As a minimum, one Initial Attack Incident Commander or a Type-6 engine with two firefighters will be sent to size up the fire and take action as needed. District or a combination of District and Refuge resources may be necessary to meet this requirement. If the fire cannot be easily seen from the road or other access point, then a helicopter will be dispatched if available, or else reconnaissance aircraft from the NPS or NCDFR will be requested. Another option is for an aerial observer to board an approved contract aircraft to scout out the fire. The resource which arrives first is responsible for providing Dispatch with an accurate fire size-up and determining an AMR. The interagency Incident Response Pocket Guide (IRPG) carried by each firefighter contains a fire size-up checklist. The AOP contains a checklist for fire size-up as well as initial attack response considerations.

Once the fire is adequately sized up and an AMR determined, the on-scene IC will request any additional resources that are needed to accomplish the AMR. A pre-determined initial attack taskforce will often be available on stand-by at Alligator River or Pocosin Lakes NWR during PL-IV and higher days and will be quickly dispatched. The closest resource concept will be utilized in all urgent wildfire dispatch operations. Refuge and cooperator resources will be requested and dispatched per the AOP, which also includes an annually updated list of radio frequencies.

Occasionally, due to the location of the fire, intense fire behavior, and/or threats to values to protect, a fire, using the NWCG Complexity Analysis, may be classified at a complexity higher than the currently responding resources are qualified to handle. At this point, the District fire management staff and agency administrator will review and begin the procedures for initiating large fire management right away.

4.1.5. Extended Attack and Large Fire Management

The Mattamuskeet Complex maintains a preparedness planning package (Appendix A) annually updated and kept at Complex Headquarters and in the DFMO's and District Dispatch's offices along with copies of this FMP. This package consists of sample analysis tools for large fires and a sample delegation of authority for incident management. It also includes a guide for Extended Attack Organization (Type 3) specific to Fire Management District 1, maps showing major values to protect and private lands within and adjacent to the Mattamuskeet Complex, and a local vendors list.

Extended attack may go far beyond the resources listed in the Appendices noted above. When wildfire incidents exceed the capabilities of the Fire Management District and local cooperators, the District Dispatch Office will coordinate orders for additional emergency resources through State and Federal area dispatch centers and the Southern Area Coordination Center (SACC).

Policies and procedures for completing incident analysis, delegations of authority, and providing incoming briefings for Incident Commanders and fire teams are found in the *Redbook*, Incident Management Information. The District Fire Management Officer will assist the Refuge Manager in completing these procedures.

In the event the selected initial attack AMR is unsuccessful, an analysis will be used to evaluate realistic alternative strategies against selected safety, environmental, social, economic, political, and resource management objectives. Through the analysis, a management alternative will be recommended for selection by the Refuge Manager. The selected alternatives will use one (or a combination) of AMR strategies to manage the incident. A new analysis will be made whenever significant changes occur that may affect the intended outcomes. The Refuge Manager will direct the Incident Commander to put together the resources to manage the incident in line with the current selected alternative.

When multi-jurisdictions are involved, the FWS will consult its partners during the Complexity Analysis process, and order the corresponding level team. Unified Command will be recommended.

4.1.6. Aviation Operations

The Mattamuskeet Complex makes use of aircraft on a fairly regular basis. All fire-related aviation operations follow applicable guidelines of the DOI National Business Center - Aviation Management Directorate. The Aviation Plan will provide local refuge aviation direction, policy and guidance that is consistent with national agency and interagency policy. It will also contain the station pre-accident plans, risk assessments, and Aviation Hazards Map. This plan should be updated every two years or as needed to update the Aerial Hazards Maps and incorporate policy changes, and can be found in Appendix B.

4.1.7. Reviews and Investigations

Reviews and investigations are used by wildland fire and aviation managers to assess and improve the effectiveness and safety of organizational operations. Brief descriptions of various reviews and associated procedures and requirements, including those for serious wildland fire accidents, entrapments, and fire trespass are listed in the *Redbook*. All prescribed fires declared a wildfire will have an investigative review initiated by the Refuge Manager. The level and scope of the review will be determined by policy and procedures of the *Redbook* and the *FWS Fire Management Handbook*.

Incident Commanders and Single Resource Bosses will ensure AARs take place in a timely manner and that any significant issues are brought to the attention of the District FMO or Refuge Manager.

A formal review of each significant initial attack and extended attack operation will be made by Agency and cooperator personnel as needed. The purpose of these reviews will be to address safety, organizational, operational, fiscal, and biological issues with regards to the wildfire.

4.1.8. Reports

Mattamuskeet Complex staff will contact the District FMO or District Dispatch Office to report all wildland fires. The District Dispatch Office will be responsible for reporting daily wildland fire occurrence to the State Coordination Center. Reporting the status of large fires through submission of an ICS-209 report will be the responsibility of the IC.

When a wildland fire chemical is applied aerially into or within 300 feet of a waterway, or is applied or spilled from ground resources directly into a waterway or within potential reach of a waterway, the IC will notify the agency administrator of the chemical application. The agency administrator will follow all reporting procedures outlined in the *Redbook*, including the completion of the Wildland Fire Chemical Reporting Form (NIFC #9210-18). Fire chemicals include long-term retardant, fire suppressant foam, wet water, and water enhancers.

The District FMO will ensure an Individual Fire Report (DI-1202) is completed and electronically filed in the Fire Management Information System (FMIS) for the following types of fires **within 10 days** of a fire being declared out:

- all wildfires on FWS and FWS-protected lands,

- wildfires threatening our lands on which we take action,

- all false alarms responded to by field office staff, and

- all converted prescribed fires. When a fire exceeds prescription, it must be converted to a wildfire and a separate new report filed to report acres burned by the wildfire from the time of declaration of wildfire to the time of being declared out.

DI-1202s are required regardless of who takes action (FWS engine, cooperator, or contractor). When FWS participates in fire suppression on lands in another jurisdiction, the agency with jurisdiction for the fire will file a report and the refuge will file an assist report to document our response and to support potential billing to non-federal entities for trespass fires. These procedures are covered in the AOP.

4.2. Hazardous Fuels Management

All fuel treatment projects (prescribed burning, herbicide, mechanical) will follow all management directions as outlined in the CCPs (FWS 2006, FWS 2008) and all applicable Department, Service, and fire management policies. A hazardous fuel project complies with NEPA requirements if (a) the field office's approved FMP or planning documents and the accompanying EA adequately discuss the action; or (b) a categorical exclusion covers the activity. If an individual proposed project does not meet the above requirements, it will require further environmental review or permits before implementation. All hazardous fuel treatments will contribute to the overall refuge management goals and objectives as outlined in Section 3.

The temperature in the world's climate is predicted to increase above natural levels in the coming decades. As the climate warms, sea levels are also predicted to rise. This could impact the coastal environments of the Mattamuskeet Complex and highlights the importance of maintaining coastal wetlands in a healthy, productive state. Use of prescribed fire and other fuel treatments will help maintain the health of these ecosystems, particularly in the marshes along the sound shores. Healthy marsh grasses hold soils in place with their root systems and catch and filter sediment during high tides or storm surges, thus reducing sound shore erosion.

Scientists have also predicted that as the earth's climate warms, the frequency and severity of wildfires will increase across the globe. The use of fuel treatments to reduce fuel loads and aid in wildfire control becomes increasingly important in minimizing the severity and rate of spread of wildfires for the protection of natural resources and of communities surrounding the refuges. District fire and Refuge staff will continue to monitor changes in the scientific community's knowledge regarding climate change/ sea level rise and adapt management decisions as appropriate.

Prescribed burning and non-fire fuel treatments all contribute to the refuge wildfire preparedness efforts. Roads, dikes, canals, and cut firebreaks provide a system of fuelbreaks on the refuges. These fuelbreaks require regular treatments such as mowing road shoulders and dikes, day-lighting canals, and cutting firebreaks to keep their effectiveness as fuelbreaks and allow cost effective maintenance.

Overall goals for habitat and hazardous fuels management are to:

1. Develop a prescribed burning regimen for all appropriate lands on the refuges in order to burn within an established fire return interval that returns fire to fire-dependent/adapted plant communities.

2. Conduct prescribed burns on an average of 10,000 acres per year while striving to burn 4 – 12,000 acres annually over the next 5 years in order to meet habitat management and fuel treatment objectives on all refuges.

3. Maintain as needed the approximately 239 acres of firebreaks, roads and dikes that compartmentalize the 78 prescribed burn units for all refuges during the 5-yr planning period.

4. Develop an understanding of the conditions in which the various sites and fuel types on the refuges can be safely burned, meet resource objectives, and meet other constraints such as smoke management guidelines.

5. Inform the public of the importance of fire as a management tool.

6. Develop the Complex's capacity for qualified, experienced firefighters to assist the District Fire Management Team to carry out the prescribed burning program. Personnel and equipment must continually be developed to meet challenges and opportunities.

Program limitations common to the Mattamuskeet Complex fuels management program include:

1. Smoke management impacts to nearby communities must be considered prior to initiating all prescribed burns. Some of the required weather conditions required for mitigating smoke impacts severely limit the numbers of burn windows during the year.

2. Weather conditions on these refuges are very difficult to predict with a high degree of accuracy and certainty due to their proximity to large water bodies.

3. Availability of aviation resources to help manage refuge lands.

4. Availability and costs for helicopters for aerial ignition and other fire management activities reduces management effectiveness.

5. A relatively low percentage of non-fire funded refuge employees have the interest or fitness levels to participate in wildland fire activities.

6. Organic soils which are prone to ignite and cause significant negative issues must always be a primary consideration before conducting prescribed burns on these refuges.

7. The remoteness of Cedar Island NWR, which takes 3-5 driving hours for FWS fire resources to reach, always increases costs and logistics for fuel management activities.

8. Wetland soils and protection considerations must be taken into account on all fire management activities.

9. Access and availability of specialized equipment capable of working in the wetland soils is always a factor in wildland fire activities.

10. Fire suppression and preparedness needs limit availability of fire resources for prescribed fire activities.

4.2.1. Prescribed Fire Program for Hazardous Fuels and Habitats

Prescribed fire planning and implementation will follow the standards and policies set forth in the *FWS Fire Management Handbook,* the *Redbook,* and the *Interagency Prescribed Fire Planning and Implementation Procedures Reference Guide 2008* (abbreviated *Prescribed Fire Guide,* www.nifc.gov/fire_policy/rx/rxfireguide.pdf).

Experience and research have shown that fire has the capacity to maintain plant and animal diversity and preserve unique plant communities that cannot exist without periodic disturbance and nutrient recycling. Many plant species have evolved around periodic fire. Frequently burned marshes often contain ten times more grass species than infrequently burned marshes if not limited by high salinities (Frost, 1995). Pine savannahs require frequent fire to release the grasses from woody brush. Longleaf pine stands require fire to maintain healthy growing and reproductive conditions. Perhaps the most common fire-adapted tree species is pond pine which requires heat generated by fire to open the cones for seed dispersal. Many pond pine stands on the Mattamuskeet Complex are threatened by a combination of southern pine beetle infestations and encroachment of other woody vegetation due to fire exclusion. For these reasons, and those explained previously, fire will be an integral key to maintain healthy ecosystems on these refuges.

The pine wetlands, pocosin, swamps, and marshes of the Mattamuskeet Complex have historically seen fire return intervals ranging from 1-3 years to decades, as evidenced by remnant vegetation types. Active fire suppression has altered natural fire regimes and contributed to an ever-increasing and potentially hazardous fuels buildup. Large tracts of cleared farm land, water bodies, road construction and drainage canals have acted as fire breaks to restrict natural fire spread.

4.2.1.1. Program Overview

Each FMU has been divided into Fire Compartments and then further subdivided into Burn Units. Approximately 40,000 acres of the Mattamuskeet Complex can be considered burnable, with 35,050 acres in fire maintained ecosystems. Based on a fire return interval of three to five years, approximately 4,000 to 12,000 acres should burn annually to maintain plant and wildlife habitat and minimize fuel buildup on the three refuges. Management flexibility is used during evaluation of the annual work plan when individual burn unit rotations can be examined to see if resource, weather, or fuel conditions warrant a more frequent or a less frequent burn interval. Water levels, weather, soil moisture, and seasonality will play a role in the scheduling of burns; therefore, the actual annual prescribed burn acreages for the refuge will vary considerably. Specific prescribed fire and fuel treatment goals are listed by FMU in Section 3.2.

Prescribed fire treatments may be conducted during any season of the year depending on the specific management objectives of the burn. Currently, the majority of the burns are conducted between October and February, but the Complex would like to expand to include more growing season burns where appropriate. While the use of prescribed fire may be desired throughout all

Figure 10: Mattamuskeet National Wildlife Refuge – Burn Units

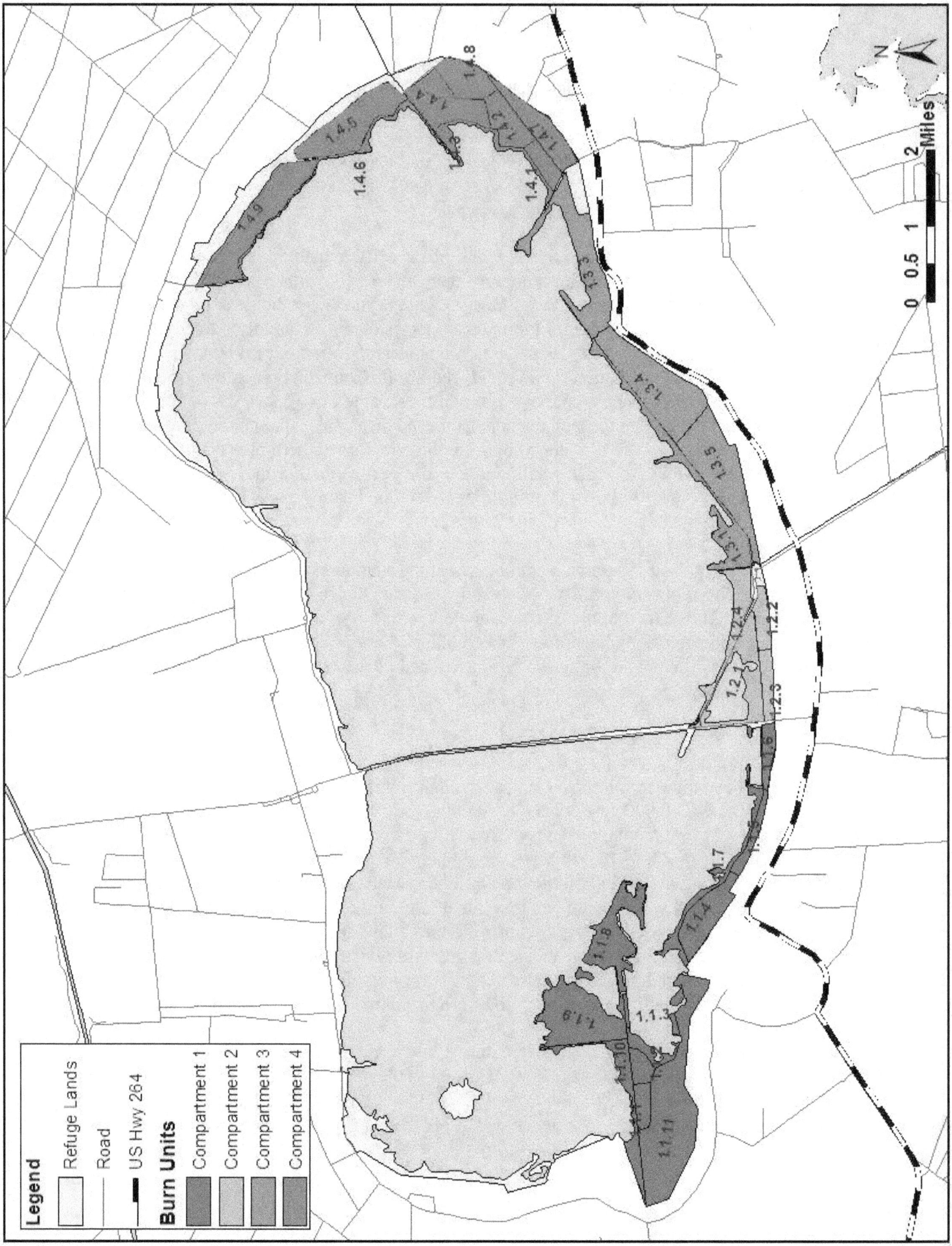
Legend
Refuge Lands
Road
US Hwy 264
Burn Units
Compartment 1
Compartment 2
Compartment 3
Compartment 4
N
0 0.5 1 2
Miles
1.4.5
1.4.6
1.4.9
1.4.1
1.3.3
1.3.4
1.3.5
1.2.4
1.2.2
1.2.1
1.2.3
1.1.7
1.1.4
1.1.8
1.1.9
1.1.3
1.1.11

seasons of the year, the combination of atmospheric conditions for excellent smoke dispersal and timing of the burn to achieve optimum fire effects on fuels or habitat do not always coincide. Considerations such as waterfowl and neotropical migratory songbird nesting or fire danger considerations can influence when an area is burned or require additional restrictions in the Prescribed Fire Plan (PFP) to lessen harmful impacts to both wildlife and habitat. Allowable burn dates will be determined by burn unit and detailed in that unit's PFP.

A 5-year average for treated unit size on all 3 refuges is 1,817 acres (range 1 to 5,000 acres). Prescribed fire complexity ranges from low to high across these Burn Units with the majority of the prescribed burns as moderate complexity (RXB2) burns. A few burns are high complexity because of WUI considerations, the complexity of the organization, or fire behavior concerns. The occasional debris burn is considered low complexity (RXB3) due to the number and organization of the resources used and the chance of escape. A PFP may include multiple complexity analyses with different complexity levels so that the appropriate complexity level may be used based on changes in burning conditions, ignition methods, or available resources.

4.2.1.2. Effect of National and Regional Preparedness Levels

There can be certain situations at local, regional or national levels which can result in prescribed burning operations on the refuge being limited or curtailed. At District Preparedness Levels IV and V, Burn Bosses must consider the Distirct's Staffing Level before igniting a burn. Resources must be available to meet criteria described in the Step-up Plan. The Southern Area Multi-Agency Coordinating Group (SAMAC), in consultation with agency fire coordinators, determines Regional Preparedness Levels based on wildland fire activity within the Southern Area and the need for fire suppression resources. At Regional Preparedness Level 4 or 5, the Regional Director must approve all prescribed burns. Prescribed fires may be ignited during National Preparedness Level 4 or 5 as specified in the *National Interagency Mobilization Guide*. National and Regional Preparedness Levels can be determined by checking the National Situation Report at: http://www.nifc.gov/nicc/sitreprt.pdf.

4.2.1.3. Project Planning

Fire and refuge management staff will develop an annual prescribed fire program of work that targets specific Burn Units in the Mattamuskeet Complex for a given year. The specific treatments within the program of work will be reviewed by the Refuge Manager or Biologist to determine the potential for conflicts between fuel management and other biological objectives. The DFMO will work with the Mattamuskeet Complex staff to address any conflicts (e.g., change in season of burn, exclusion of management area, etc.) in the Prescribed Fire Plans (PFP). A red wolf Biologist will always be contacted prior to burns on Mattamuskeet and Swanquarter NWRs, but particularly close coordination is needed for burns conducted during the red wolf whelping season (March – June) to determine potential impacts to dens.

Based on the annual program of work, the District FMO and/or PFS will assign Mattamsukeet Complex or District staff to develop the PFPs for the applicable Burn Units. The PFPs should ideally be prepared and developed by an interdisciplinary team in which at least one member has successfully completed the Service's Prescribed Fire Planning and Implementation course or the

Figure 11: Swanquarter National Wildlife Refuge – Burn Units

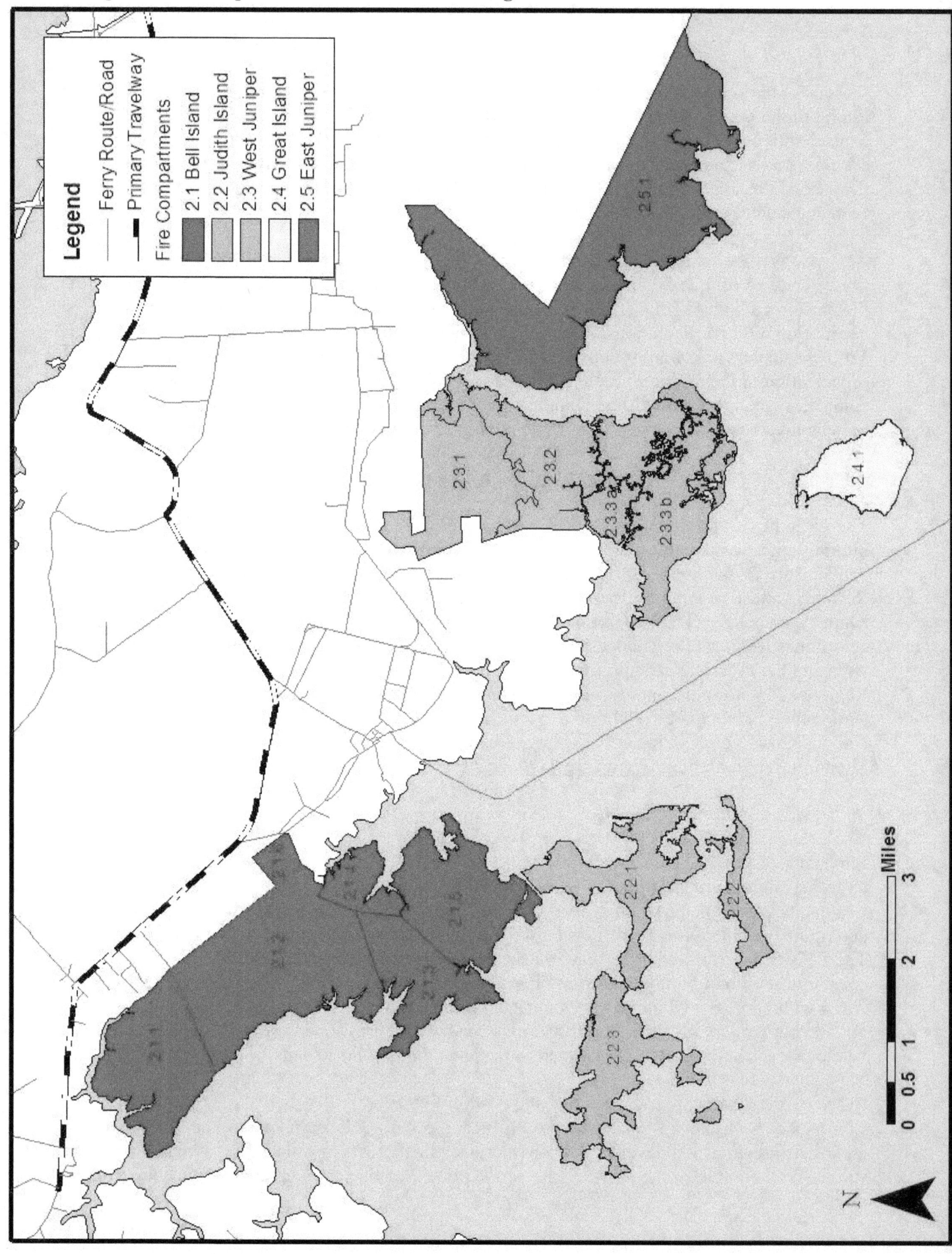

Legend

— Ferry Route/Road

━ ━ Primary Travelway

Fire Compartments

- 2.1 Bell Island
- 2.2 Judith Island
- 2.3 West Juniper
- 2.4 Great Island
- 2.5 East Juniper

NWCG Prescribed Fire Burn Boss training courses. All prescribed fires must have a written plan that is reviewed and approved by the Refuge Manager, District FMO, and reviewed by another qualified Burn Boss for technical accuracy. The PFPs will follow the template and guidance in the *Prescribed Fire Guide*, Service, and regional policy.

Several other constraints influence project planning on the refuges. Utilizing appropriate wind direction to keep smoke off the highways and safety for the public and firefighters on the highways are major concerns for prescribed burning at all 3 refuges. Risk of ground fire and escaped fires are the dominant factors influencing the use of prescribed fire in organic soils and pocosin shrub habitat. Size of the burning compartment and access within the compartment are additional issues that have to be addressed as a prescription is prepared. The compartment must be sufficiently broken down into manageable burn units in order to meet smoke management guidelines. Access to the compartments must be adequate to ensure the safety of firefighters and deployment of contingency forces. The Refuge and District fire organizations must be available and ready with completed burn plans, specified resources for operations, and contingencies whenever burn windows occur.

4.2.1.4. Project Implementation

Upon approval of the burn plan, burn unit preparation can begin. Prescribed fire preparation activities may include identifying and preparing containment lines around the burn unit perimeter. Special considerations for holding and firing will be minimized by pre-burn activities such as raking around snags along the fire breaks or mechanical removal of heavy fuel accumulations near structures or other areas of high fiscal or resource value. Preparatory burns, as discussed in the PFP, may be used to take advantage of wet conditions within the blocks and treat the fuels along the edges exposed to the wind and sun in advance of the main burn. Any pre-burn treatment that can be completed to improve the safety and effectiveness of the burn will be explored and implemented.

During the development of the PFP, the number of operational and contingency resources are determined and documented. All Service personnel on a prescribed burn will be NWCG or Service qualified for the position that they are assigned. Cooperators, contractors, and casual hires (AD) may be used to implement prescribed fires. ADs must meet FWS standards. Cooperators, such as members of Volunteer Fire Departments, must have appropriate qualifications certified by their agency. Those who supervise FWS employees during prescribed fires must meet FWS standards. The Service recognized Prescribed Fire Crew Member (RXCM) position, with a moderate fitness rating, may be used on refuge lands under procedures outlined in the *FWS Fire Management Handbook*. The approved exception form is included in the Appendix. Since the RXCM qualification cannot be used for suppression, all PFPs will address the use of RXCM in relation to contingency resources.

A Burn Boss, qualified at the appropriate complexity level will be in charge of implementing the prescribed burn in accordance with the approved Prescribed Fire Plan. This includes any public or agency notifications, completion of the Go/ No-Go Checklists, smoke management requirements, obtaining spot weather forecasts, and conducting an operational briefing. Cooperators must be contacted and often must be available to participate at the operational

Figure 12: Cedar Island National Wildlife Refuge – Burn Units

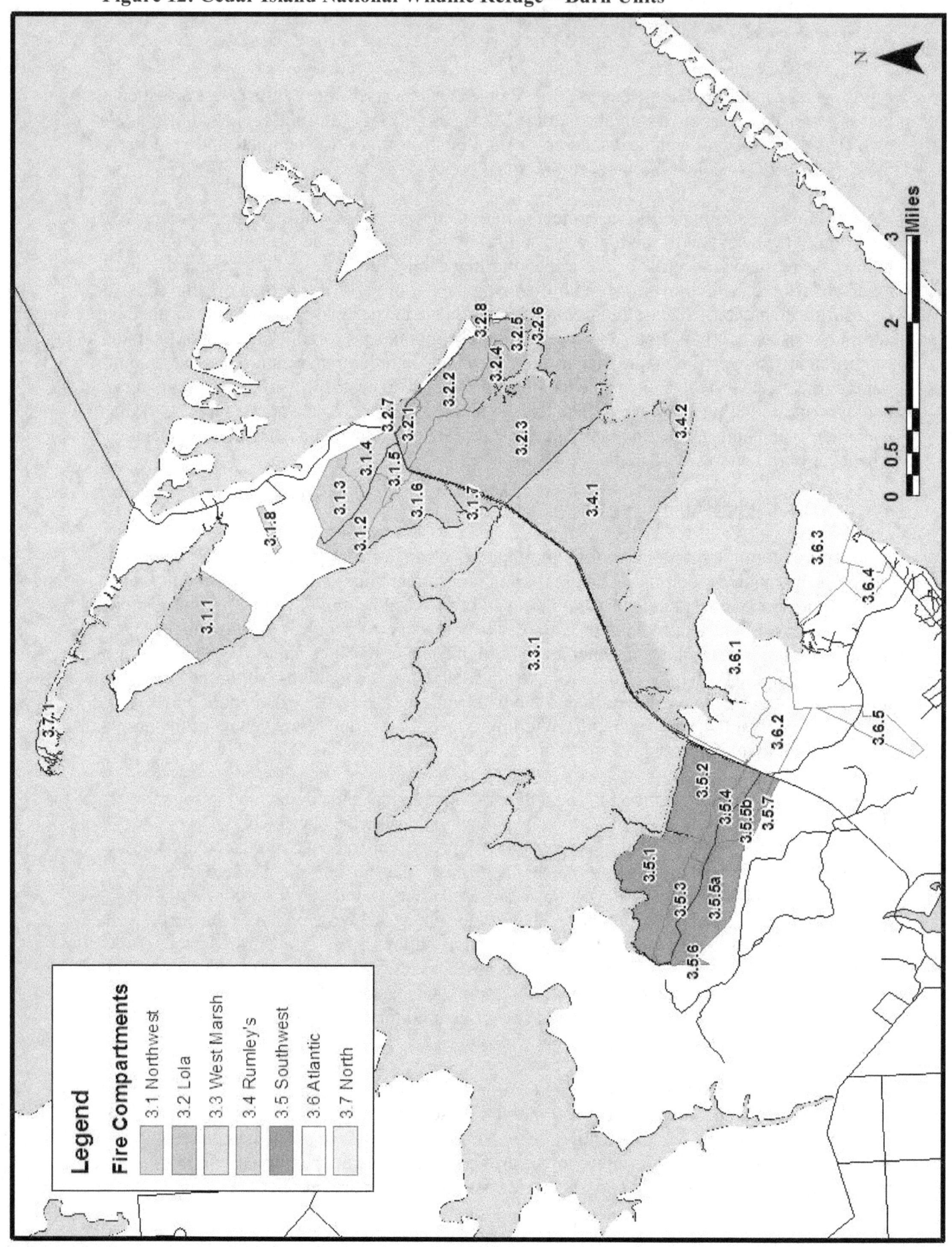

Legend

Fire Compartments

3.1 Northwest
3.2 Lola
3.3 West Marsh
3.4 Rumley's
3.5 Southwest
3.6 Atlantic
3.7 North

Miles
0   0.5   1   2   3

and/or contingency levels. Availability of helicopters and other specialty equipment must be assured. The presence or availability of contingency resources is an element within the Go/ No-Go checklist.

The public will be informed of prescribed fires through news releases, interpretive messages, and educational programs. Individual prescribed fires should not be conducted without informing those agencies and members of the public likely to be impacted.

A prescribed fire will be converted to a wildfire by those identified in the burn plan when that person(s) determines that the contingency actions have failed or are likely to fail and cannot be mitigated by the end of the next burning period. A prescribed fire will be converted to a wildfire when the fire has spread outside the project boundary, or is likely to do so, and cannot be contained by the end of the next burning period. A prescribed fire can be converted to a wildfire for reasons other than an escape. AMR will be made to such incidents and a formal analysis (Complexity and WFSA) undertaken as required by policy. The Refuge Manager will be notified of an escaped prescribed fire, as identified in the burn plan.

4.2.1.5. Smoke Management

Combustion releases gases into the air including carbon monoxide, carbon dioxide, hydrocarbons, and small quantities of nitrous oxide. These emissions generally have little negative effect on air quality. However, the release of small particulate matter (PM) can affect air quality and contribute to regional haze. PM smaller than 2.5 microns in diameter tends to lodge in the lungs, causing health problems, especially for those who already have respiratory problems. Fires also result in a slight increase in the pH and organic and mineral matter in the underlying soils. The Hyde County Commissioners have identified smoke management and the potential for smoke to cause traffic accidents as their primary concern regarding implementation of a prescribed burning program in the Mattamuskeet Complex.

The refuges must comply with all applicable Federal, State, and Local air pollution control requirements, as specified within Section 118 of the Clean Air Act, as amended (42 USO 7418). To do this, refuges must take aggressive action to manage smoke from prescribed burns to minimize impacts and maintain air quality. Since fires are not point sources, but rather tend to be spatially distributed singular events, temporary impacts to visibility must be recognized, expected and managed. All refuges are required to obtain necessary permits for prescribed fires, comply with the national ambient air quality standards (NAAQS) both inside and outside refuge unit boundaries, and protect visibility in Congressionally-mandated Class I areas. These are federally mandated programs that are enforced nationwide with program implementation primarily carried out by state and local air quality agencies. Swanquarter NWR is the only Class I area in the District. Prescribed burning can be conducted in this Class I area when the quality of visitor experience has been considered in the planning and implementation of the burn. Because of the relatively short duration of smoke impacts to visibility during prescribed burns, the impact to the visitor experience is minimal and best managed when considered with other SSA in the smoke management section of the PFP.

Smoke management is always a major consideration when smoke-sensitive areas (SSA) such as communities, hospitals, airports, and highways are nearby. During the writing of a PFP, a smoke management map will be prepared that shows the location of all critical smoke sensitive areas within 20 miles of the proposed burn. During burning, strategies and tactics will be used that minimize smoke production as a public safety hazard. The appropriate tactics for a Burn Unit will be discussed in the Smoke Management section of the PFP where the SSAs will be classified by sensitivity to visibility or particulate matter concentration and actions developed to address them. Figures 13 and 14 show generic smoke hazards maps for the refuges. The *Smoke Management Guide for Prescribed and Wildland Fire* (2001) is a useful reference for PFP preparers. Examples of possible smoke management tactics are:

- Mop up within 50 feet of any control line adjacent to major roads or residential areas.

- Place smoke ahead signs along any public road that may have visibility impaired by the fire's smoke.

- Notify law enforcement agencies if visibility is impaired along any public road.

- Position law enforcement personnel at appropriate locations to alert motorists of smoke impacted areas.

- Ground fire will be aggressively extinguished if it becomes a threat to air quality to the extent refuge management directs.

On the day of the burn, the fire weather forecast will be evaluated to ensure that the burn can proceed within prescribed weather parameters, including atmospheric conditions for smoke dispersal. All PFPs shall include the following minimum smoke management considerations:

1. Identified SSAs in the Smoke Management Section of the PFP will be addressed in light of predicted weather and atmospheric conditions. Wind direction and velocity shall either provide for transport of smoke and pollutants away from critical SSAs, or the smoke will be adequately diluted or dispersed before reaching the SSAs. Smoke dispersion models such as V-Smoke or Blue-Sky/RAINS are recommended for this analysis.

2. NCDFR Smoke Management Guidelines (SMG) will be followed unless an Operational Evaluation Burn (OEB) is implemented.No burning shall be undertaken if an authorized governing agency has issued an air pollution health advisory, alert, warning or emergency for the refuge or surrounding metropolitan areas.

3. Burn Bosses will use the firing techniques and timing that minimize smoke impacts to the public and accomplishes the burn's objectives.

4. Smoke will be monitored during prescribed burns. If smoke threatens a SSA, the appropriate authorities will be notified and conditions monitored to assess potential impacts.

Figure 13: Smoke Hazard Map

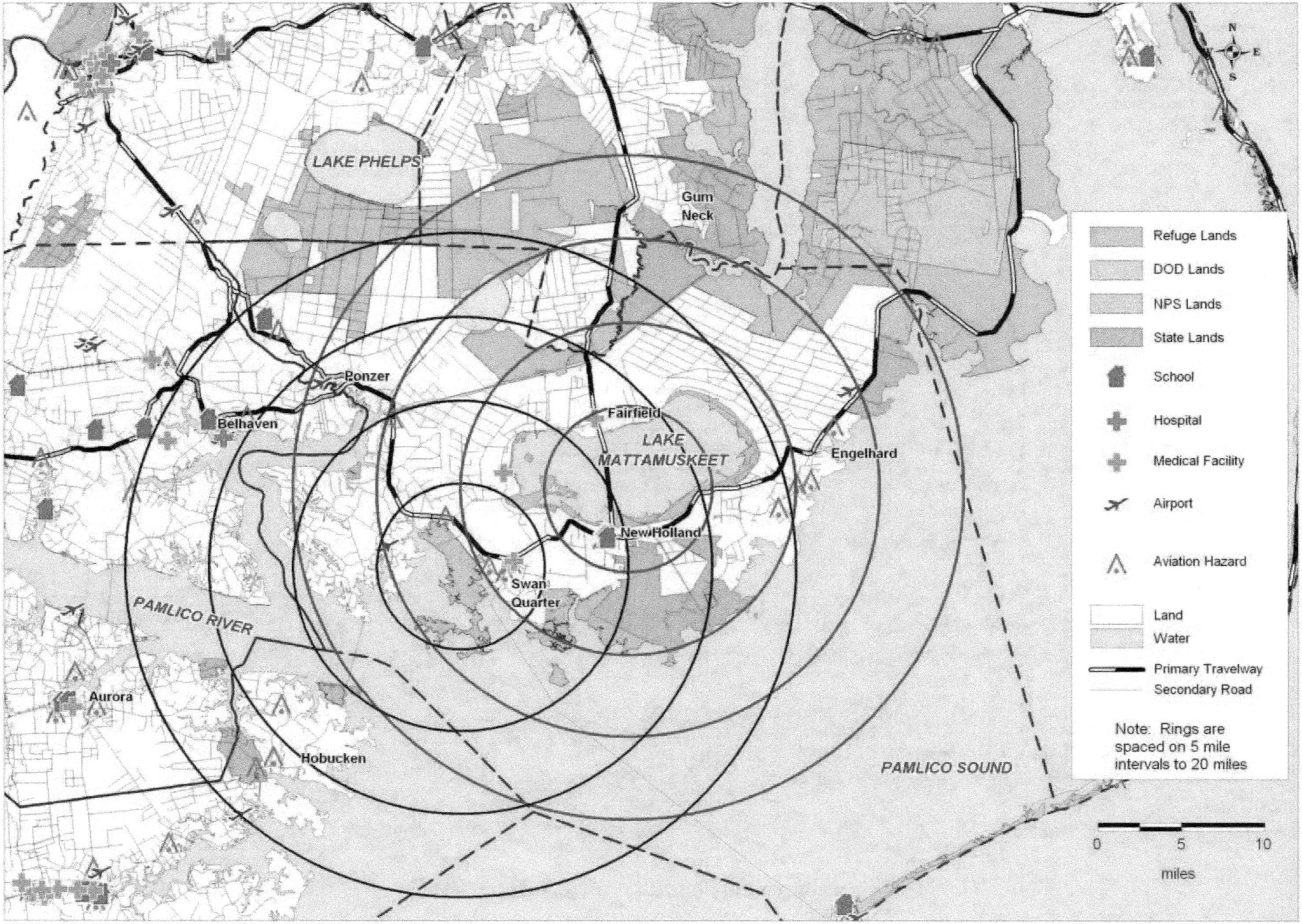

Legend:

Refuge Lands
DOD Lands
NPS Lands
State Lands
School
Hospital
Medical Facility
Airport
Aviation Hazard
Land
Water
Primary Travelway
Secondary Road

Note: Rings are spaced on 5 mile intervals to 20 miles

miles
0 5 10

PAMLICO SOUND

PAMLICO RIVER

LAKE PHELPS

LAKE MATTAMUSKEET

Gum Neck

Fairfield

Engelhard

New Holland

Swan Quarter

Ponzer

Belhaven

Hobucken

Aurora

Figure 14: Smoke Hazard Map

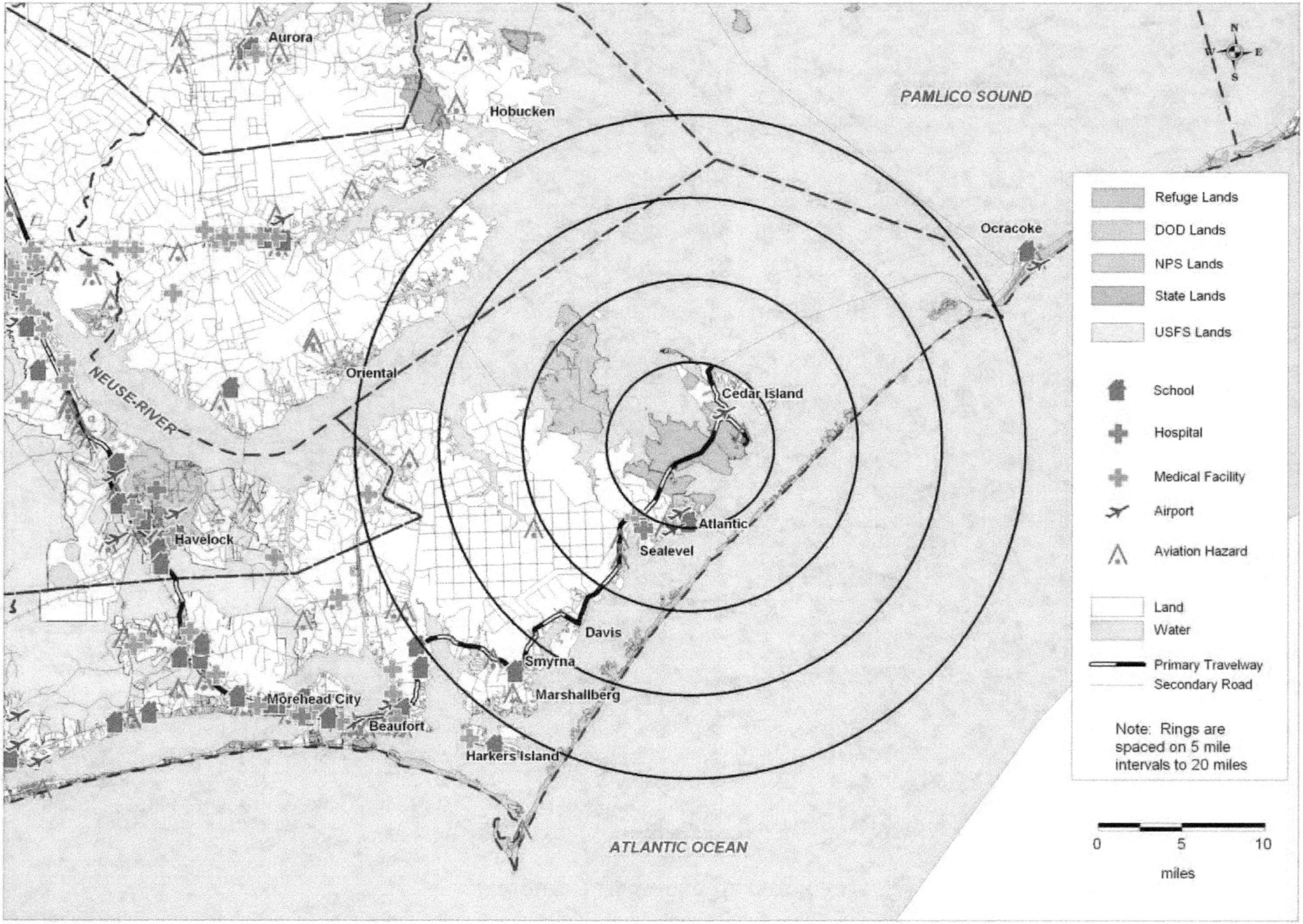

Legend:
- Refuge Lands
- DOD Lands
- NPS Lands
- State Lands
- USFS Lands
- School
- Hospital
- Medical Facility
- Airport
- Aviation Hazard
- Land
- Water
- Primary Travelway
- Secondary Road

Note: Rings are spaced on 5 mile intervals to 20 miles

miles: 0   5   10

PAMLICO SOUND

ATLANTIC OCEAN

NEUSE RIVER

Ocracoke
Cedar Island
Atlantic
Sealevel
Davis
Smyrna
Marshallberg
Harkers Island
Hobucken
Oriental
Aurora
Havelock
Morehead City
Beaufort

4.2.1.6. After Action and Escaped Fire Reviews

The Burn Boss will ensure an informal After Action Review (AAR) is conducted for each operational period on a prescribed fire *(Redbook,* Chapter 17). This AAR will focus on performance standards to enable agency administrators and firefighters to discover for themselves what happened, why it happened, and how to sustain strengths and improve on weaknesses. Certain events or a culmination of events that may affect future prescribed fire implementation and/or policy should be submitted via the Rollup documentation (found at http://www.wildfirelessons.net). The questions to answer in conducting an AAR are:

- What did we set out to do (what was planned)?
- What actually happened?
- Why did it happen that way?
- What should be sustained? What can be improved?

All prescribed fires converted to a wildfire will have an investigative review initiated by the Refuge Manager. The level and scope of the review will be determined by policy and procedures of the *Redbook* and the *FWS Fire Management Handbook.*

4.2.1.7. Reports

The completion of an approved PFP is the primary documentation that a prescribed fire has been attempted or completed. The PFP will specify information to be included in the project file. Various documents that record weather data or public comments may be attached to the completed plan, which includes a record of observed fire behavior and the kind and amount of resources committed to the burn. The Burn Boss will document the conditions under which the burn was conducted in order to evaluate how closely the prescribed fire conformed to planned fire behavior, what unanticipated difficulties were encountered during the action, and how well the prescribed fire accomplished the desired results. All completed burn plans and associated documents will be kept in a binder with the District PFS as a permanent record of the burn day activities.

On the day of the burn, the District Dispatch Office will notify NCDFR that a prescribed burn is planned and provide that person with the size, time of ignition and the location of the burn. Within **ten days** following the completion of a prescribed burn the Burn Boss will ensure that an Individual Fire Report (DI-1202) has been electronically submitted into the Fire Management Information System (FMIS). Prescribed fire accomplishments must also be reported to the National Fire Plan Operations and Reporting System (NFPORS) in the same time frame as FMIS. The District Dispatch Office will also be responsible for reporting daily prescribed burning activities to the State Coordination Center.

When a wildland fire chemical is applied aerially into or within 300 feet of a waterway, or is applied or spilled from ground resources directly into a waterway or within potential reach of a waterway, the Burn Boss will notify the agency administrator of the chemical application. The agency administrator will follow all reporting procedures outlined in the *Redbook*, including the completion of the Wildland Fire Chemical Reporting Form (NIFC #9210-18). Fire chemicals include long-term retardant, fire suppressant foam, wet water, and water enhancers.

4.2.2. Non-fire Hazardous Fuels Treatment Program

4.2.2.1. Overview

The reduction of hazardous fuels contributes favorably to refuge management objectives and includes not only prescribed burning, but also mechanical and herbicide treatments. Past non-fire fuel treatments have been largely mechanical and included firebreak construction and maintenance, mowing road shoulders, and small thinning treatments around structures. Herbicide treatments on the refuges have focused on invasive species control, but have not been coordinated as fuel treatments. These efforts are being better organized and documented between programs as both hazardous fuel and resource objectives are being met. In the future, herbicides may also be used to treat vegetation in firebreaks to improve the efficiency of mowing to manage vegetation and reduce maintenance costs.

The ten-year annual average for reported non-fire fuel treatments on the Mattamuskeet Complex is 4.3 treatments for 42.3 acres. As project reporting and coordination between refuge program areas continues to improve and the use of non-fire fuel treatments expands, the Mattamuskeet Complex will see a jump in the number of acres treated by non-fire methods. Table 9 summarizes the projected annual WUI and non-WUI non-fire fuel treatments for the next 5 years on refuges in the Complex.

Table 10: Projected Annual Non-Fire Fuel Treatments

Refuge	WUI acres	Non-WUI acres
Mattamuskeet	70	412
Swanquarter	17	0
Cedar Island	56	20
Total	143	432

District fire and refuge management staff will develop an annual program of work that targets specific treatment areas. Non-fire treatments may be conducted during any season of the year depending on the specific management objectives. Herbicide treatments will use only refuge approved herbicides documented in a Pesticide Use Proposal. All non-fire fuel treatments will be coordinated with other refuge program areas and CCP step-down plans, such as Invasive Species Management Plan, to increase efficiency of treatments and decrease any administrative or biological conflicts. Specific treatments within the program of work will be reviewed by the Refuge Manager or Biologist and may be reviewed by other subject matter experts if necessary.

Projects are generally moderately complex in terms of planning and implementation with most of the complexity involving the specialized mechanical equipment needed to hold up on organic or wetland soils. A variety of equipment is utilized in non-fire fuel reduction activities. Typical equipment may include mowers, chippers, grinders, roller choppers, dozers, and mulchers. Herbicides could be applied using back-pack sprayers, the marsh master, or aircraft. Specialized equipment that better meets the needs and protects refuge resources and sensitive sites are continually being developed, tested and employed as appropriate.

Within **ten days** following the completion of a non-fire fuels treatment, refuge staff will contact the District Dispatch Office to ensure that a web-based fire report will be electronically submitted into FMIS. Non-fire accomplishments must also be reported to NFPORS in the same time frame as FMIS. In addition to the fuels reduction project accomplishments being reported in NFPORS, an annual pesticide report is required to document the application of specific herbicides, biological agents, and active ingredients.

4.2.2.2. Treatments

Mechanical fuel reduction activities will be used as needed and where appropriate to reduce hazardous fuel accumulations in firebreaks, roads, refuge administrative sites, visitor use areas and wildland-urban interface areas. Herbicide applications may also be used to kill or retard vegetative growth on these sites as well as target invasive species. Prescribed fire and non-fire techniques may be used individually or in tandem to provide the best resulting effect in the fuel reduction effort.

The Fire Management Units have been divided into Burn Units whose boundaries are delineated by roads, constructed firebreaks, canals, and dikes. The network of roads, dikes and firebreaks on the three refuges not only makes prescribed burning possible, but it also is very important for wildfire control. Mowing roads and/or road shoulders is an important mechanical treatment for control of hazardous fuels. Firebreak maintenance is done annually primarily using mechanical means, but any method (herbicides, mechanical or burning) may be used if appropriate. Occasional mechanical treatments to day-light the ditches to remove overhanging vegetation is also important for wildfire control. Regular mowing of dikes on the refuges is also important for wildfire control.

Some Burn Units can be difficult to access safely or in a timely manner. Future mechanical treatments for hazardous fuels may simply be access improvement projects that would allow fire staff greater access to a Burn Unit for prescribed burning and thereby increase the safety and efficiency of that project, or improve access to an area for control of wildfires. Such projects might include installation of culvert crossings or bridges or the cutting of short access routes. Other mechanical treatments in the next 5 years may include thinning and mulching vegetation around refuge housing, public use facilities, or other administrative areas to increase their protection from wildfires. WUI mechanical projects in and around communities would increase defensible space. In areas where smoke management severely restricts the potential for using prescribed burning to reduce hazardous fuels, non-fire treatments may be used to achieve management objectives. Any fuel thinning or biomass removal projects must carefully consider impacts to wetland, organic soils. Low ground pressure, tracked equipment generally results in the least impact to the root mat, but can greatly increase the cost of work.

The invasive species control efforts on the refuges not only benefit the habitat, but also create a fuel model change. Phragmites is the primary non-aquatic target for control and is generally considered a Fuel Model 4. Successful control would result in a Fuel Model 3 with restoration of the native marsh grasses. Herbicide treatments are the first phase of Phragmites control, but these treatments are then often followed up with a prescribed fire treatment. Firebreak maintenance on the refuges may also include herbicide treatments to improve the efficiency of mowing, reduce woody vegetation, and reduce maintenance costs.

4.2.3. Process to Identify Hazardous Fuels Treatments

The objectives identified in the National Fire Plan and in the *10-Year Comprehensive Strategy* result in a range of specific strategies identified in this plan. The Southern Wildfire Risk Assessment (SWRA) can be used to categorize the risk of wildland fire to communities, and this document addresses strategies that contribute to protection of those communities in the vicinity of the refuges. Projects in the WUI receive the highest priority (see Figures 15 - 17). District fire staff will work collaboratively across the District and in coordination with our fire management partners to prioritize fuels projects in the District and on each refuge.

The Mattamuskeet Complex has collaborative relations for fire management operations with the NC Division of Forest Resources, the NC Wildlife Commission, The Nature Conservancy, the US Forest Service, the Department of Defense, local volunteer fire departments and adjoining counties' Emergency Management offices. Partners are consulted during project development for areas of collaboration and efficiencies.

4.3. Emergency Stabilization and Rehabilitation

The US Fish and Wildlife Service takes responsibility for taking prompt action to determine the need for and to prescribe and implement emergency treatments to minimize threats to life or property or to stabilize and prevent unacceptable degradation to natural and cultural resources from the effects of a wildfire on refuge lands (*Redbook* 2008). Damages resulting from wildland fires are addressed through four post wildfire activities: wildfire suppression activity damage repair, emergency stabilization (ES), burned area rehabilitation (BAR), and long-term restoration. Departmental and Service emergency policy and guidance for these post wildfire activities are found in the *Redbook* (2008), *620 DM 3, 095 FW 3.9*, and the *Interagency Burned Area Emergency Response Guidebook* (2006). District fire staff will attempt to coordinate and/or inform our fire management partners on our activities. There have been no previous ES and BAR treatments on the Complex.

4.3.1. Wildfire Suppression Activity Damage Repair

Wildfire suppression activity damage repairs are planned actions taken to repair damages to resources, lands, and facilities resulting from wildfire suppression actions, and are documented in an Incident Action Plan. These actions are usually implemented immediately after the containment of the wildfire by the Incident Management Team before the Team is demobilized. If necessary, engineers, hydrologists or other specialists will be consulted to determine the extent of damages incurred to refuge resources and facilities from suppression activities.

Mattamuskeet NWR Wildland Urban Interface

Legend

Mattamuskeet NWR
Wildland Urban Interface
Community Polygon

State Recognized CAR
Fairfield
Lake Comfort
Lake Landing
New Holland
Swan Quarter

SWRA CAR

MeanWFSI
low
medium
high
very high

The community polygons for the Southern Wildfire Risk Assessment (SWRA) Communities at Risk (CAR) are from the published results. The SWRA CAR polygons served as a starting point for the State Recognized CARs (recognized March 15, 2006 by NCDFR) that were digitized using 2006 color aerial photographs. The SWRA CARs and mean WFSI (wildfire susceptibility index) values were derived from the risk assessment in the program and are not federally recognized.

Swanquarter NWR Wildland Urban Interface Areas

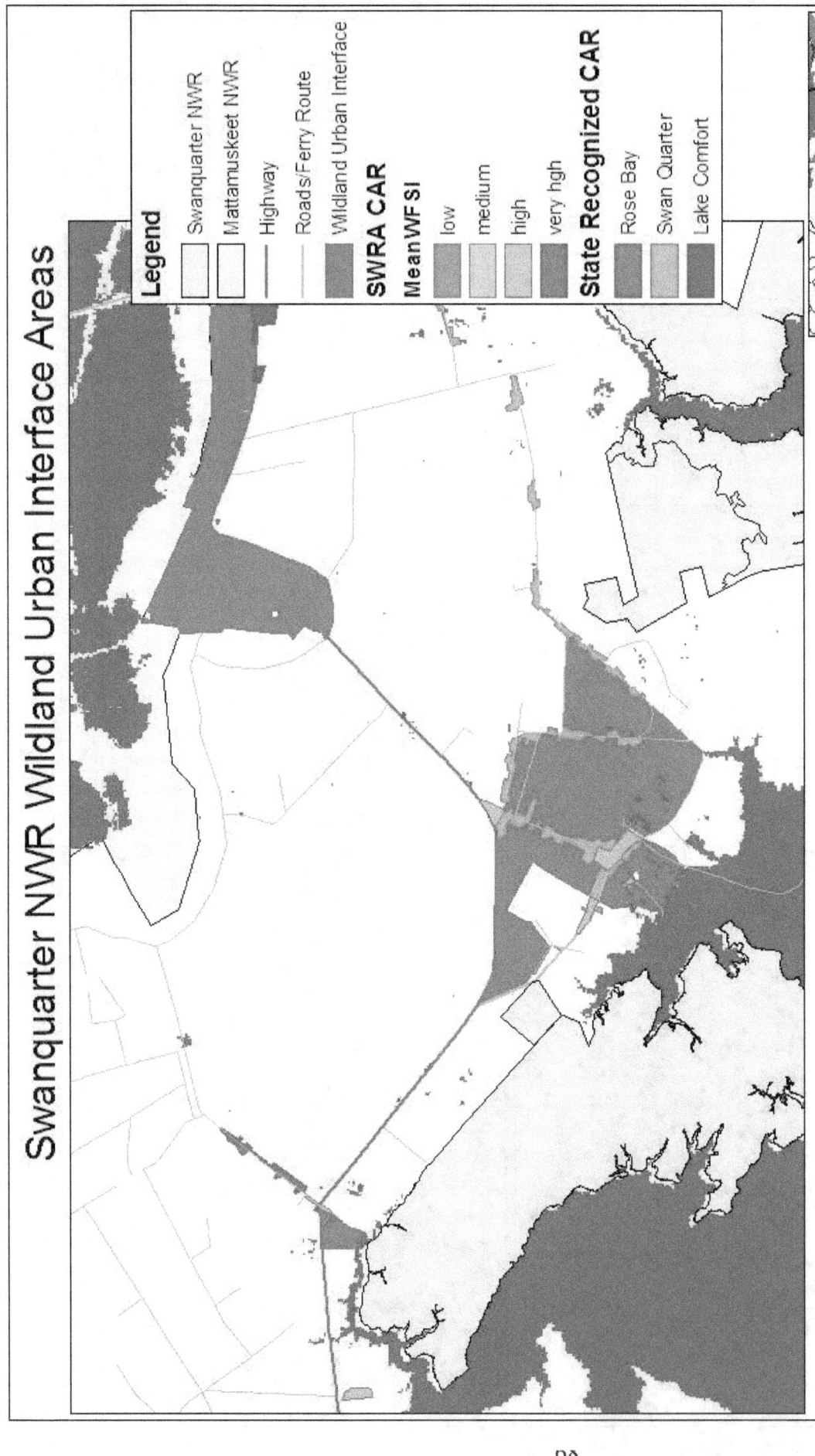

Legend

- Swanquarter NWR
- Mattamuskeet NWR
- Highway
- Roads/Ferry Route
- Wildland Urban Interface

SWRA CAR

MeanWFSI
- low
- medium
- high
- very hgh

State Recognized CAR
- Rose Bay
- Swan Quarter
- Lake Comfort

The community polygons for the Southern Wildfire Risk Assessment (SWRA) Communities at Risk (CAR) are from the SWRA published results. The SWRA CAR polygons served as a starting point for the State Recognized CARs (recognized March 15, 2006 by NCDFR) that were digitized using 2006 color aerial photographs. The SWRA CARS and the Mean WFSI (wildland fire susceptibliy index values for them that were not derived from them were derived from the risk assessment in the program and are not federally recognized.

Cedar Island NWR Wildland-Urban Interface Areas

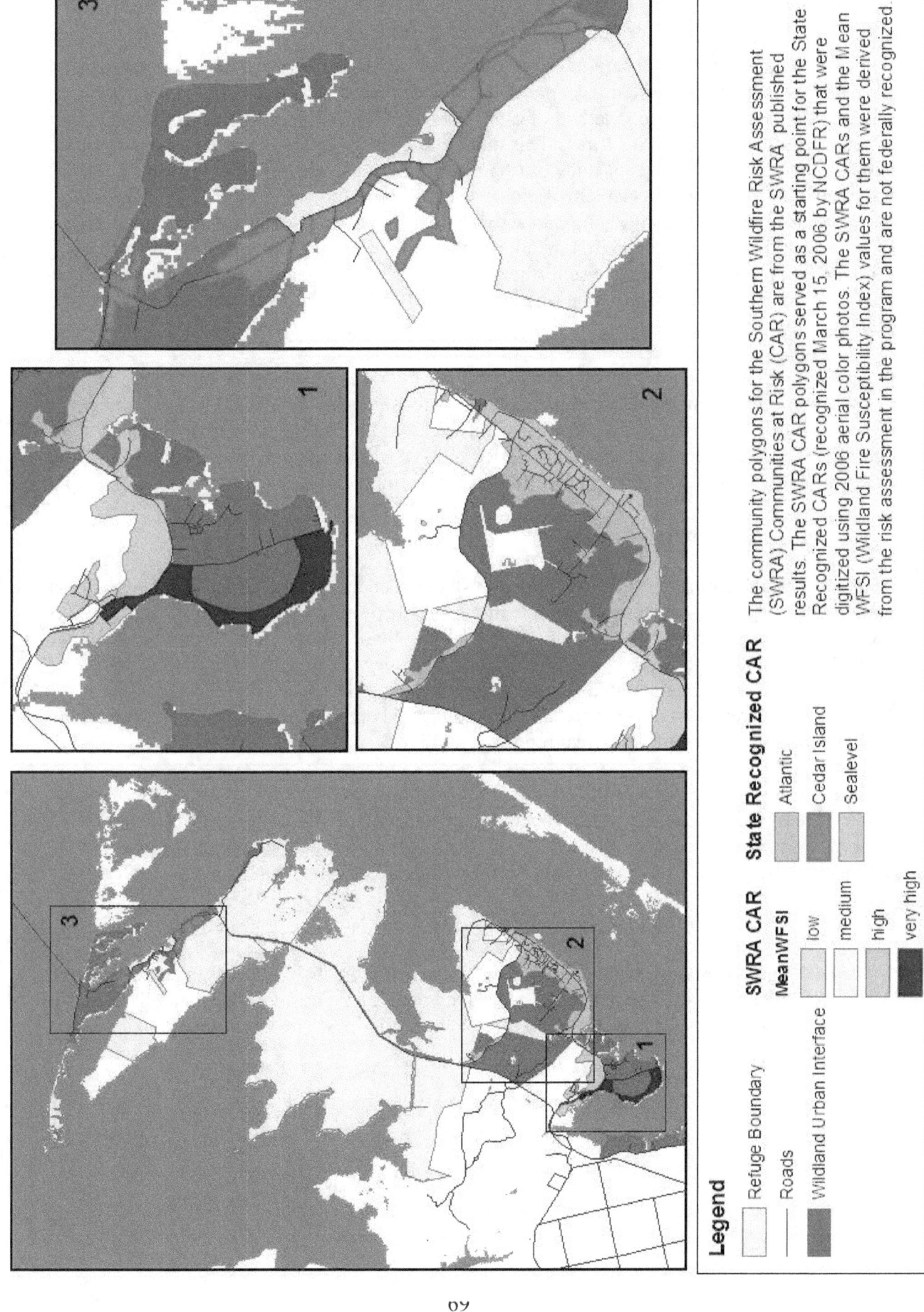

Legend

Refuge Boundary

Roads

Wildland Urban Interface

SWRA CAR

MeanWFSI

low

medium

high

very high

State Recognized CAR

Atlantic

Cedar Island

Sealevel

The community polygons for the Southern Wildfire Risk Assessment (SWRA) Communities at Risk (CAR) are from the SWRA published results. The SWRA CAR polygons served as a starting point for the State Recognized CARs (recognized March 15, 2006 by NCDFR) that were digitized using 2006 aerial color photos. The SWRA CARs and the Mean WFSI (Wildland Fire Susceptibility Index) values for them were derived from the risk assessment in the program and are not federally recognized.

Following every suppression action on the refuge that requires the use of hand tools or control lines or causes other surface damage, the affected sites will be repaired. The tractor-plow unit will remain the most common method of establishing firelines to serve as control lines on initial attack operations on refuge wildfires. This method is the most effective and efficient resource in suppressing wildfires in areas of thick brush and organic soils. However, the resulting line, if left open and exposed to the elements, can cause accelerated oxidation of organic soils and be more prone to ground fire following the next ignition. Following every fire on the refuges, plow lines and hand lines will be repaired by pulling the berms back into the line in areas where utilizing equipment would not cause further damage. In most cases, firelines in marsh will be a combination of walk-down lines (smashed vegetation) and wet lines that will not require rehabilitation.

Grass seed will not normally be sown on plow lines, but rather they will be allowed to re-vegetate naturally. Emergency seeding and control techniques will be used in areas where erosion control is necessary (e.g.; heavily disturbed areas like ICPs, parking areas, pump sites, and etc). Wetlands will be protected as needed. Snags will be removed if they pose a threat to life or property, but otherwise preserved for cavity nesting wildlife.

4.3.2. Emergency Stabilization (ES)

Emergency stabilization are planned actions to stabilize and prevent unacceptable degradation to natural and cultural resources, to minimize threats to life or property resulting from the effects of a wildfire, or to repair/replace/construct physical improvements necessary to prevent degradation of land or resources. ES actions must be taken within one year following containment of a wildland fire and documented in a Burned Area Emergency Response Plan (BAER Plan). Monitoring for treatment effectiveness will be conducted on all approved treatments and the results described in an annual or final report.

Natural recovery is the preferred ES treatment for the refuges. No specific actions have been undertaken to date to stabilize an area or implement a BAER Plan; however, it is recognized that under certain possible scenarios, stabilization treatments could be implemented. Allowable actions permitted on the refuge that may be deemed necessary to stabilize an area under an emergency response include:

1. Assessments:
   - Burned area assessments will identify post-fire threats to federally listed or proposed threatened and endangered species and what, if any, cost effective stabilization measures can be implemented to prevent further post-fire condition degradation.

2. Cultural Resources:
   - Site stabilization and Protection
   - NHPA Section 106 Compliance

3. Non-native Invasive Control:

- Assessments to determine the need for treatment. Contingent upon location of known infestations, possibility of new infestations due to management actions, and suspected contaminated equipment use areas.

- Treatments to prevent detrimental invasion by non-native species (not present on the site).

- Treatment of invasive plants introduced or aggravated by the wildfire. The treatment objective when the population is aggravated is to maintain the invasion at no more than pre-wildfire condition.

- Treatments to prevent permanent impairment of designated Critical Habitat for Federal and State listed, proposed or candidate threatened and endangered species.

4. Re-vegetation:

- Stabilize a site and minimize water or wind erosion.

- Reduce invasion of non-native invasive plants.

- Prevent Critical Habitat for federally listed threatened and endangered species from being more impaired than if nothing was done.

- See *Interagency Burned Area Emergency Response Guidebook* (2006) for further information.

5. Federal Field Unit Infrastructure:

- Emergency stabilization of improvements and minor facilities (e.g., signs, kiosks, guardrails, and others as listed in Section 3) burned or damaged by wildfire is appropriate only for public health and safety reasons. If it is not an immediate threat to public health, it will be reviewed under the Burned Area Rehabilitation Plan

- HAZMAT and Facility Assessment and Stabilization

- Emergency Road Repairs and Maintenance - Road closure is preferable unless the road is needed to provide immediate access to essential activities (e.g., hospital and post office access, threatened and endangered species management, communication systems). Damages due to suppression activities to roads will fall under "Wildfire Suppression Damage Activity Repair" as stated above.

6. Burned Area Emergency Response Team (BAER TEAM) and Plan Development:

- An ad-hoc team of Agency Administrator (Project Leader), refuge staff and any additional personnel necessary will form an initial Burned Area Emergency Response Team. If warranted, a National BAER Team will be ordered to meet the refuge's needs. The team, under the guidance of the Agency Administrator will:

  a. determine the need for burned area assessments

  b. determine what further expertise is needed to conduct assessments

  c. develop a Burned Area Emergency Response Plan with identified treatments

d. Track treatments in NFPORS

e. implement treatments

f. monitor effectiveness of treatments

g. write report based on monitoring results including a final report

4.3.3. Burned Area Rehabilitation (BAR)

Rehabilitation refers to efforts taken within three years of containment of a wildland fire to repair or improve wildfire-damaged lands unlikely to recover naturally to management approved conditions, or to repair or replace minor facilities damaged by wildfire. These efforts are documented in a separate Burned Area Rehabilitation Plan (BAR Plan).

Natural recovery is the preferred rehabilitation treatment for the refuges. No specific Burned Area Rehabilitation Plans have been implemented to date following wildfires; however, it is recognized that under certain possible scenarios, rehabilitation treatments could be necessary. Allowable actions permitted on the refuge that may be deemed necessary to rehabilitate an area following wildfires include:

1. Cultural Resources:

    - BAR funds are used to ensure burned area rehabilitation treatments conform to Section 106 of the National Historic Preservation Act (NHPA). Funds can not be used for restoration of any cultural resource or heritage sites.

    - Additional limitations are listed in the *Interagency Burned Area Emergency Response Guidebook* (2006).

2. Non-native Invasive Control:

    - BAR funds can be used to control non-native invasive plants in burned areas only if an approved management plan and existing program is in place addressing non-native species control.

    - Remaining allowable actions are the same as ES – see above.

3. Re-vegetation:

    - Allowable actions are the same as ES – see above.

4. Forest Management:

    - Forest management may be considered if the ecosystem is unlikely to recover naturally from wildfire damage (not regenerate for 10 years following fire) as prescribed by a certified silviculturalist. The use of BAR funds to plant trees must be addressed in an approved land management plan (see *620 DM 3*). Tree planting is limited to the following:

      a. facilitating the succession and stabilization of forest ecosystems.

      b. reestablishing habitat for federally listed threatened or endangered species, or other special status species.

c. reintroducing or reestablishing native tree species (i.e. Atlantic White Cedar) and seed sources lost in a stand replacement fire.

5. Minor Facilities:

- The repair or replacement of minor improvements and facilities (e.g., kiosks, fences, interpretive or boundary signs, recreation facilities, trails, permanent long-term monitoring plots or other as) burned or damaged by wildfire to pre-fire specifications is authorized with the use of BAR funds only if these improvements or facilities are necessary for implementing an approved land management plan. It does not include the construction of new or upgraded facilities that did not exist before the fire. BAR treatments and maintenance of BAR improvements beyond 3 years from wildfire containment is funded with other program funding. Minor facility repair or replacement must be addressed in the BAR plan.

6. Burned Area Rehabilitation Team and Plan Development:

- An ad-hoc team of Agency Administrator (Project Leader), refuge staff, and any additional personnel necessary will form a Burned Area Rehabilitation Team. The team, under the guidance of the Agency Administrator will:

  a. Allowable actions are the same as ES – see above

4.3.4. Long Term Restoration

Restoration includes continuing the rehabilitation beyond the initial three years or the repair or replacement of major facilities damaged by the wildfire. Land management plans and other funding sources are available to continue the rehabilitation efforts beyond three years.

4.4. Prevention, Mitigation and Education

The *Master Agreement* states that all parties will work cooperatively on prevention and education efforts. District fire staff will attempt to coordinate and/or inform our fire management partners on our activities.

4.4.1. Prevention/ Mitigation

The inadvertent or intentional ignition of wildland fuels by humans is illegal. The objective of fire prevention activities is to prevent human-caused wildfires, which are not a significant ignition source for the refuges. The most common human-caused wildfires for Mattamuskeet NWR are escaped debris burns that burn from private property onto the refuge. Fire prevention programs in the area are typically presented by the NCDFR. Mattamuskeet Refuge Complex or District staff will assist in specific fire prevention efforts in coordination with NCDFR to address specific occurrences or arson outbreaks. We will investigate all human-caused wildfires at the earliest possible time. The investigation may range from a documented determination of cause by the initial attack crew to criminal investigation by a qualified arson investigator.

4.4.2. Education

Our outreach goal is to enhance knowledge and understanding of wildland fire management policies and practices through internal and external communication and education. The education programs will emphasize the importance of prescribed fire and fuels management in both preventing wildland fire and as a management tool to meet refuge habitat objectives. Community education programs will also include steps area residents and property owners can take to reduce possible damages to their homes and property from wildfires through programs such as Firewise. These education efforts may take the form of school or civic programs, refuge displays, news releases, or handing out fire education materials at public events.

Fire operations on the refuges can be very noticeable, and questions from the public about what is happening and how it concerns their welfare are to be expected. The District must be prepared to protect the public during fire operations and inform them of the purpose and techniques of our fire management program. The refuges and District will continue to promote public understanding of wildland fire, both the natural role of fire in the ecosystem and the associated risks of living in that environment. Refuges and the District will promote community assistance through education and coordination with county planning and zoning departments to promote firewise construction and landscaping principles and initiatives in fire-sensitive land use planning. In addition, efforts would be made to explore the initiation or facilitation of WUI Councils or Firewise/Firesafe organizations in communities surrounding the refuge. Outreach and public education efforts by the refuge fire management program will supplement other refuge outreach programs.

Opportunities will be sought to inform the public of significant wildfire incidents through local, state and national media. During such incidents, a Service and/or NCDFR Public Information Officer will be appointed to maintain media contacts. Departmental, Service, and refuge fire management policy will be expressed and facts given concerning the incident. Cooperative relations with other agencies will also be highlighted as appropriate. to educate the public on the cooperative and efficient system of firefighting. When appropriate, a dual message should be presented that informs the public that the Service will apply an Appropriate Management Response to all wildfires, yet will use prescribed fire to reduce the threat of wildfires and manage resources. Through the judicious use of managed fire, better habitat for wildlife can be created while maintaining fire-influenced ecosystems and improving forest health. The primary message to convey to the public is that the Service takes a proactive approach to wildland fire which includes the use of fire as a management tool.

5.0. Monitoring and Evaluation

5.1. Fire Management Plan

5.1.1. Annual FMP Review

This FMP will be reviewed annually and updated as needed, upon local agency administrator approval. A checklist of FMP elements included in the appendix will be initialed by the DFMO and signed by the Refuge Manager to ensure that a yearly review has been completed. Revisions of FMPs with Regional review and concurrence are required every five years. FMPs may be revised more frequently if significant changes on FWS or adjacent lands occur or following completion of a new or significantly revised CCP or habitat management plan.

5.1.2. Fire Management Plan Terminology

Terms in the FMP are defined in the National Wildfire Coordinating Group, located at http://www.nwcg.gov/pms/pubs/glossary. Any terms used in the FMP and not found in the glossary are defined below.

High Reliability Organization (HRO) - an organization that has succeeded in avoiding catastrophes in an environment where normal accidents can be expected due to risk factors and complexity.
> Wikipedia contributors, 'High reliability organization', *Wikipedia, The Free Encyclopedia*, 28 September 2008, 06:16 UTC, <http://en.wikipedia.org/w/index.php?title=High_reliability_organization&oldid=241479620> [accessed 15 October 2008]

Point protection - Providing direct protection with available resources to a single defensible value at risk.

5.2. Treatment Effectiveness

5.2.1. Fire Effects Monitoring

During all prescribed burns, periodic weather and fire behavior observations will be made and recorded. The Prescribed Fire Burn Boss will complete an evaluation of each prescribed burn. This evaluation will include the information on weather and fire behavior, a narrative of firing procedures, smoke behavior and/or problems, a cost analysis of the burn, and any significant equipment problems. The evaluation will also assess to what degree the objectives of the burn were met, and any recommendations for future burns in that particular Burn Unit. The effects of prescribed burns should be monitored by a combination of the fire management staff and biological staff.

District fire and refuge staff should work towards developing a first order fire effects monitoring plan by 2011. This step-down plan will provide a monitoring protocol that will help determine if prescribed burn objectives were met. Monitoring results could influence the fire return frequency, fire ignition techniques, and prescription parameters. The plan would follow Service and Regional guidance on plan development.

Non-fire fuel reduction activities are typically designed to reduce the level of hazardous fuels and to alter vegetation structure and composition to meet refuge resource objectives. Post-treatment assessment will include documentation of fuel reduction and vegetative change in NFPORS and FMIS, including whether the treatment met resource objectives. Individual non-fire fuel treatments may require specific measurements to determine treatment effectiveness. These should be identified during project development and assessments included in the project file.

5.2.2. Prescribed Fire Research

There are many gaps in our knowledge of the role of fire in freshwater and brackish marshes, pine forest savannahs, pocosin and pond pine wetlands as well as other associated wetland ecosystems in the coastal plain of North Carolina and other states on the eastern seaboard. Research is needed increase our knowledge of the historic role and the management of fire in these fire-dependent ecosystems, as well as what changes should be anticipated in light of climate change and sea level rise. Research focal areas include:

- Fire effects on breeding and wintering secretive marsh birds in irregularly-flooded brackish marshes and freshwater marshes.

- Moist-soil and brackish marsh plant responses to prescribed fire for the benefit of migratory birds.

- Tonnage of particulate matter released by freshwater marsh, brackish marsh, small-depression pocosin and other habitat types for the lower coastal plain of North Carolina.

- Fire effects on the amphibian and reptile communities on the Mattamuskeet Complex.

- Effectiveness of prescribed fire to create openings in emergent vegetation for migratory birds.

- Developing new and fine tuning existing products for modeling and predicting smoke behavior and plume development.

- Understanding fire effects in areas affected by sea level rise.

- Understanding fire effects on carbon sequestration in the various coastal ecosystems.